"From what has just been said it must be obvious to every sane-thinking person that the first task necessary for the real education of man is to develop in each separately formed centre the natural need to blend simultaneously the functions of one part with the others, in order that the manifestations of these three parts, formed separately according to the laws of nature in man's general psyche, and which inevitably demand a separate education, may be harmoniously united, and may, in the period of responsible life, work together according to their normal capacities."[1]

Man—A Three-brained Being

Resonant Aspects of Modern Science and the Gurdjieff Teaching

Keith A. Buzzell

© 2007 Keith A. Buzzell

Second edition, 2007
This second edition has been revised and redesigned from the first edition (*Man – A Three Brained Being*, Maine: Wyllaned, 1997). In addition, chapter 4 has been rewritten and expanded.

ISBN # 0-9763579-2-5
Responses via the author, editors or the publisher are welcome.

KEITH A. BUZZELL
499 UPPER RIDGE ROAD
BRIDGTON, ME 04009 USA

FIFTH PRESS
444 EAST 200 SOUTH
SALT LAKE CITY, UT 84111 USA
WWW.FIFTHPRESS.COM

Other books by Dr. Keith A. Buzzell
> *The Children of Cyclops: The Influence of Television Viewing on the Developing Human Brain.* Fair Oaks: AWSNA Publications, 1998.

> *Perspectives on Beelzebub's Tales.* Salt Lake City: Fifth Press, 2005.

> *Explorations in Active Mentation.* Salt Lake City: Fifth Press, 2006.

Man—A Three-brained Being

Resonant Aspects of Modern Science and the Gurdjieff Teaching

Keith A. Buzzell

Editors: John Amaral, Marlena Buzzell,
Bonnie Phillips, Toddy Smyth

Fifth Press, Salt Lake City

FOR ALL OUR CHILDREN
AND GRANDCHILDREN

Contents

INTRODUCTION 1
Are the times we are living in different? We have new images, some
born of invention, with conflicts in the timings of their digestion.
We are rapidly losing time-to-think and time-to-come-into-relationship.
This loss threatens human survival.

CHAPTER 1 11
NEW CONCEPTS
The view of our life as tri-brained, which entered with Gurdjieff circa
1915 and was recapitulated in the 1950s by science, is a perspective
capable of reconciling human values and new technologies. In Gurdjieff's
'hydrogens', electromagnetic bonding energies are delimiters of material
states, from massless to mass-based, which helps us understand both life
and brain function, including 'psychic and spiritual matters'. In his view
of 'worlds', the quantum nature of our Universe is inferred, involution
and evolution may be seen as motions and reconciliations of time,
and the triadic nature of consciousness and conscious
transformation may be studied.

CHAPTER 2 27
THE TRIUNE BRAIN
Primarily for survival, brains initially create images from blendings of multi-dimensional sensory images concerned with multiple material levels and ranges of vibration, from which meanings are derived. In the second brain, this leads to the emergent sense-of-self with its difficulty of separating inner sensation from interpersonal life. The third brain creates abstract images of outer and inner life, deriving principles from them and initiating action. Its hazards concern the power to also build images which are non-resonant with life. New perspectives, such as the scientific method and the Gurdjieff Work, provide hope for reconciliation of this condition.

CHAPTER 3 61
CONSCIOUSNESS AS THE COALITION OF IMAGES
The biological appearance of brained life, capable of digesting images and reconciling time, of witnessing life itself, of self-determined movement through three-dimensional space and the memory of it, represented a Great Turning. Elemental blended awareness was enhanced by the sense-of-self-other of the second brain and the sense-of-I of the third brain. Eventually, third brain consciousness could abstract each brain's hunting for what?, how? and why?. Thus, the human third brain, when it demonstrates its complete and successively appearing hierarchy of capacities, unfolds an image which is a step-by-step model of the scientific method of inquiry.

PREFACE TO CHAPTER 4 89

CHAPTER 4 91
THE DIGESTION OF FOOD, AIR AND IMPRESSIONS:
A METAPHOR FOR HUMAN TRANSFORMATION
Three-brained digestion is an octavic process requiring directed attention. Each brain extracts meaning from impressions, which intentional digestion makes increasingly coherent. This feeds and grows the sense of self-other, wherein the acts of self-remembering and self-observation cultivate a re-emergence of Conscience and a separate witnessing 'presence'. When personal effort is made, a process of confrontation and verification is set in motion, leading to growth of *being*, and the appearance of Will or I. This may be further transformed, through work on self with others, special exercises, compassion and service, into egoless I AM and possible return to higher levels of existence.

GLOSSARY 133
RECOMMENDED READING — REFERENCES 135
AUTHOR'S BIOGRAPHY 138

"You will understand this cosmic law also in all its aspects when, as I have already promised you, I shall explain to you in detail all the fundamental laws in general of World-creation and World-existence."[II]

"Even though the realms of religion and science in themselves are clearly marked off from each other, nevertheless there exist between the two, strong reciprocal relationships and dependencies ... the situation may be expressed by an image: science without religion is lame, religion without science is blind."[III]

Introduction
Man – A Three-brained Being

In 1996 I flew to London from Boston for the second time. I shared this adventure with some three hundred travelers, including a number of small children and babies. After finding my assigned place, I noticed on the back of the seat in front of me that a telephone was embedded and, if I had wished, I could have had an in-flight conversation with my son in Virginia. A large TV monitor hung from the ceiling several rows ahead, showing a safety message on how to leave the aircraft in the event of some unlikely disaster. Two seats over, a business-suited gentleman glanced at his digital watch and opened up his laptop computer. Next to me, my wife plugged in plastic earphones, set them in her ears and began to explore the dials. Events were not going well in Bosnia and Ireland and she had been reading about both in a news magazine she had bought in the airport. I turned and looked out of the window onto a bank of smoothly contoured clouds some five miles below. In my lap, the manuscript of a partially completed paper on the structure of *Beelzebub's Tales* lay open.[1]

---

1 Gurdjieff, George Ivanovitch, *All and Everything/First Series*,
  "An Objectively Impartial Criticism of the Life of Man,"
  or *Beelzebub's Tales to His Grandson* (Aurora: Two Rivers Press, 1993)
  an exact facsimile republication, of the first edition, as prepared for publication
  in English by the author, unrevised; or (New York: Penguin Arkana, 1999).
  Herein, referenced as *Beelzebub's Tales* or *The Tales*.

Associatively, my mind was drawn to the many external changes that had taken place in our world since Gurdjieff's death in 1949. Several questions emerged: Were they all of the same order of change that had occurred during his lifetime? Were there any developments that were really *new* – in the sense that a previously unexplored dimension of law had been penetrated into and had begun to show some practical results? Are modern communications and the means of travel simply extensions of past developments – operating faster and larger but not in an essentially different way? Alternatively, has *something* entered the life of humanity that is fundamentally different? I recalled Beelzebub's comment in the chapter, "France,"

> "During this time, no difference whatsoever has arisen between those three-brained beings of this planet, who existed nearly a hundred of their centuries ago, and the contemporary ones."[2]

Nothing in my own life experience had ever contradicted Gurdjieff's summary statement of "no difference." Yet, as I sat there on the 747 some seven miles above the Atlantic Ocean, the question of whether a *newness* had entered the life of mankind persisted. Looking around the cabin, I asked myself, "What is there in this typical 1996 setting that could be seen as really new which has entered man's life?" People appear to react interpersonally in the same way. The irritabilities, values and aims, concerns and enthusiasms seem unchanged. Airplanes are bigger and faster, radios and telephones are both more convenient and more complex. These appear to be direct extensions from past knowledge and past technologies – or are they? Is there anything in this newness – the advent of television and the computer, of satellites and LCD watches, of cell phones, jets and CD ROMs – that is an expression of a new-found dimension of law? If there were a new order, then, even though humans would have not fundamentally changed in the separate worlds of their triune (three-in-one) brains, the circumstances within which they live would have changed dramatically. That order of change would challenge the whole of man's evolutionary history by introducing stresses and opportunities never before encountered.

The need for an answer to my question kept prodding, poking beneath the surface of the multitude of new things that surrounded me while I was trying to feel the outline of such a new dimension of law. From somewhere within me, there was produced a sense of its having to do with *motions* that had been understood only partially, or not at all, in the relatively recent past. The answer, or the *image* that seemed to contain the germ of the answer, came in the expression, "the merciless Heropass."[3]

---

2 Gurdjieff, *Beelzebub's Tales*, p 674.
3 Gurdjieff created this expression "the merciless Heropass" as a way of approaching an understanding of time and the complex nature of our world. See *The Tales*, chapter 16, "The Relative Understanding of Time," pp 121-33 and elsewhere throughout the book.

Gurdjieff's many references to *time*, its relativity and its primary role in "the forced need to create our present existing 'Megalocosmos',"⁴ gives it a significance equal to his other conceptions, (e.g., Etherokrilno and Kundabuffer).⁵ "The merciless Heropass" refers, broadly, to the flow of time. It is the "Ideally-Unique-Subjective-Phenomenon"⁶ which results from comparable cosmic phenomena occurring within a given level of the Universe. In a fundamental sense, we have come to understand the concept of the merciless Heropass as *the infinite potency for all possible motions.*⁷

With "Heropass" as the defining context, I began to look at the changes surrounding me on this epitome of technology – the jumbo jet. What *new motions* were reflected into our environment? What could be so new as to represent a new dimension of law? Moreover, even if really new, could it have anything specific to do with the Gurdjieff Work and the potential for accelerated transformation?

As I looked about at each technological object, I restated the question of its origin, the cause of its origin, its history, its qualities and attributes, etc.. While considering the cause of its origin, I began to identify a germinal *something* shared by each of these objects, namely, that without the technological application of the principles of relativity and quantum mechanics, *none of these objects could exist.* Realizing this, I knew that I had seen *new motions* of the Heropass as a new dimension of manifested law.

The penetration of science into the micro- and macro-worlds (into their form, sequence and relative velocities) has opened man's awareness to these *new* motions (new to us but *not* newly-created). The perceptual shift that accomplished this entry was contained in relativity theory and quantum mechanics. Just as the sudden entry of a *three*-dimensional perspective on space/time energized the birth of the Renaissance and the ensuing appearance and development of science up to the close of the 19th century, the entry of a *four*-dimensional space/time perspective in this century has energized a quantum shift in man's views on all and everything.

There appears to be more than serendipity involved in the simultaneous appearance of Gurdjieff as a teacher (circa 1913) and the published insights of such men as Planck, Bohr, Einstein, Schrödinger and Hubble. Superficially, the perspectives of 20th century science and of Gurdjieff appear to be dramatically different and yet, it is our contention that both *herald* a startlingly new view of our Universe.

The primordial gulf that separates them derives from Gurdjieff's insistent and balanced incorporation of the physical, emotional and intellectual

---

4 Gurdjieff, *Beelzebub's Tales*, p 749 and Keith A. Buzzell, *Perspectives on Beelzebub's Tales* (Salt Lake City: Fifth Press, 2005), chapter 1, "The Enneagramatic Nature of *Beelzebub's Tales.*"
5 Gurdjieff, *Beelzebub's Tales*, (Etherokrilno) p 137; (Kundabuffer), pp 88-9.
6 Ibid., p 124 and further.
7 Keith A. Buzzell, *Explorations in Active Mentation: Re-Membering Gurdjieff's Teaching, A Grandchild's Odyssey* (Salt Lake City: Fifth Press, 2006), chapter 10, "In The Beginning," pp 157-63.

aspects, (i.e., the material, *being*-values and purposes) of this new perspective into one harmonious *whole*. Science, claiming no competence in the arenas of human values and purposes, is nonetheless the potent force carrier of these *new motions* with respect to the material world and a major qualifying influence on mankind's philosophical and spiritual views on the Universe.

One result of relativity theory and quantum mechanics is that, since 1949, the year Gurdjieff died, our ordinary sensate world has been profoundly interpenetrated by two additional orders of worlds:

△ the 'world within our world'—of atomic and nuclear particles and energies; of wave/particle dualities and probabilities; of quantum orbital; mass/energy equivalence and,

△ the 'world beyond our world'—of a sun's nuclear fusion; of other galaxies; of the expansion of the Universe; of supernovae, black holes and unified field theories.

In the decades from 1900 to 1950, these germinal insights remained almost the exclusive domain[8] of the theoretical and experimental scientist, largely being a fictional plaything for the general population.[9] In the 1950s, however, the technological effluent of those seminal years began to flow into the general life of humanity and became, in a remarkably short time, a tidal wave of unmeasured power and influence.

Results of the New Motions

The entry of these *new motions*–of the quantum and relative worlds–has irrevocably altered the outer and inner landscape of all life on Earth.[10] More significant than the external changes are those that have influenced the inner world of man, primarily with respect to the *functional form and sequence* of his brains. A few examples of this impact will help to clarify our theme.

From the distant time when brained beings first appeared on land, the differentiation and refinement of the external senses has had high survival priority. While the capacity to form resonant representations, or *images*, of portions of the matter/vibrations external to a creature's body can be understood as one of the crowning achievements of brained life, this capacity

---

8 Analogous to the early Renaissance, there were many artists and philosophers who explored this new landscape–among them T. S. Eliot, Pablo Picasso, e.e. cummings, Igor Stravinsky and A. L. Whitehead.

9 The stunning exception is the atomic bomb. Even here, the secrecy surrounding its development kept it tightly within a small community of scientists and military strategists.

10 Without the application of quantum and relativity principles in technology, we would not have modern television, the computer, the internet, fiber optics, weather satellites, cell phones or CD's, nor would we have the Hubble telescope, CT and MRI scanners, genetic splice replication, a host of modern pharmaceuticals, alloys and superconductors. The human genome would still be an uncharted mystery and the biochemistry and neuronal networks of the brain would be almost entirely hidden from view. How would their absence affect your life?

has one focal vulnerability – namely, that the image created by the brain must be taken as *real* – otherwise its survival value would be nullified.[11]

This imperative – to trust that an image is real – can be traced in neural, ganglionic and reflexive elaborations throughout one-, two- and three-brained life. For approximately the past two and a half million years (est.), it has continued to be both a life-saving and enabling *imperative for three-brained beings*; deeply entwined and essentially unalterable within the sensory-reflexive-motor pathways of the brain.

The technological application of man's initial understanding of electromagnetism (in the early radio, phonograph and motion pictures) began to expose that vulnerability. For the first time in evolutionary history, a *moving* and prefabricated (pre-created) image in sound, vision or both could be projected into the brain. The years 1900 to 1950 brought refinements to the techniques of image projection but it was not until television appeared that the *new motions* of relativity and quantum mechanics were revealed. Since 1950, the survival-created vulnerability of the brain has been explored and/or exploited by any person or group with a message. The prefabricated image has become a neurological 'Trojan horse'.

We have only fragmentary understandings of how our human brain processes a television signal. In view of the strands of evidence (see below) that point out the differences in the form and sequence of the neural processing of a TV signal from the neural processes taking place in reading, conversation and physical activity, the indifference and dismissive attitude of the research community is astonishing.

- ~ The sensitivity (vulnerability) of the limbic (second) brain to facial image is known.
- ~ The nullification of the alerting reflexes of pupillary change, lens accommodation and eye scanning movements is known.
- ~ The reality of non-flicker based seizure disorders in children watching television is known.
- ~ The activation of dynamic metabolic changes, (e.g., in heart and respiratory rate, hormonal release and blood flow) while *no* physical activity is enjoined is known.
- ~ Differences between the form and sequence of radiant and reflected light sources are known.[12]

When we recall that the entirety of the brain's sensory-associative-motor evolution[13] underpins the events noted above, then it appears that ignorance of how a television signal is processed by a brain, but permitting it anyhow, is more than a bit like our introduction of tons of DDT into our external

---

11 A moment's hesitation – "is it or isn't it?" – would be a fatal flaw in the evolutionary flow of life.
12 Keith A. Buzzell, *The Children of Cyclops: The Influence of Television Viewing* (Fair Oaks: AWSNA Publications, 1998).
13 Buzzell, *Perspectives*, pp 53-55.

environment before we researched its potential effects on life processes. We are now over fifty years post-introduction of both and the question of impartial research, particularly in the case of the neurophysiology of television viewing, comes immediately up against a multi-billion dollar industry and over-whelming public/political dependencies.

Related questions appear with respect to the electronically produced imaging technologies (computer terminals, video games and the internet). From their first appearance, they have been understood as if they were 'the same as' past inventions, in terms of how our brain deals with them. Our brain, however, has evolved within a constant environment of images of real events, with our sensory-motor systems honed by real survival. To plunge our brain into a sea of unreal, titillating and unfulfilled images goes beyond a failure to ask questions; it invades, it expands into activities that include arrogant manipulation and profiteering.

Each of our brains (the 'physical', 'feeling' and 'thinking') needs to be fed. The quality and quantity of its food and the timing of its introduction are critical. Food for a brain (as a sensory-associative-memory-motor-neural mechanism) is not at all the same as it is for the rest of the body. The brain lives on neural impulses, from perceptions to impressions. Each of our three brains has a large arena of impressions that are appropriate to it alone. In many events, the past impressions of each brain become major modifiers of *meaning*. Many parts of the brain require an intense period of repeated behaviors in order to develop properly. Failing the early reinforcement of appropriate impressions, the part of the brain responsible for integrating behaviors simply doesn't arborize its connections and remains not only more fixed and reactive, but also establishes many wrong connections. Much familial, interpersonal and social mayhem derives from this failure of *timing*. The uncaring and thoughtless intrusion of the technologies deriving from relativity and quantum principles has greatly impacted the biologically determined times of brain maturation.

It has been understood for a long time that there are many developmental *windows* in the human, (e.g., the closure of the neural tube, the differentiation of the digits of the hand and foot). If development is not completed in a given period, the body does not back up and do it over. Rather, it continues its surge toward overall completion and makes compromises around the uncompleted parts. Driven by the same biological imperative, the brain does very much the same. The price to be paid, however, is in the irrevocable diminishment of the possibilities of each of the three brains individually and of the three-in-one triune brain. The technological effluents of the principles of quantum mechanics and relativity function in times that are instantaneous, when compared to neural processing time. For the growing and extremely vulnerable brain, it is always *now* (the image on the screen, the computation, the reward) but the *now* of the technological products has no relation to the present moment of first-, second- and third-brain growth, development and mature function.

Introduction

Prior to the Industrial Revolution and extending to my own youth, there was a large arena of shared skills, knowledge and practice within most communities. For example, cobblers, stonemasons, blacksmiths, carpenters, mechanics, farmers and jewelers all shared manual skills that could be commonly understood and transferred 'sideways'. One recognized and respected the fundamental principles of another's work. While this common ground began to fragment with the Industrial Revolution, it had almost completely disappeared by 1950.

Presently, I can move through three days, interact with a hundred and fifty people and talk with *no one* who understands how their home heating system, plumbing, radio, TV, computer, fax, car or telephone works. Even college graduates have vacant gaps in their understanding of simple physical and electrical principles. Gaps of this size have become more wide-spread today and have created greater vulnerabilities in day-to-day life than have ever existed in the past. They are vulnerabilities of the first (physical/core/reptilian) and second (limbic/emotional/mammalian) brains in particular, as the foundation of self-confidence and of a normal sense-of-self derives from the normal development of these brains. One end-result (perhaps the most pervasive and crippling), is the increasing inability on the part of many people to take care of themselves — both with respect to acquiring skills which can be applied to useful, wholesome work and to taking care of their health through appropriate diet, exercise and close relationships with others. The recent tragedies associated with hurricanes and tsunamis are dramatic testimony to these deficiencies of responsiveness to the needs of others.

As a society, we are rapidly losing time-to-think/ponder and time-to-come-into-relationship. Surrounded by communication linkages and pre-created images that operate at close to the speed of light, the vulnerability of the brain to instantly completed images has significantly subverted what is an essentially biological *process*, which can only operate harmoniously in its own corresponding time.

To think into a question, to explore its interstices and get the *measure* of it, is a process which moves in neural time – definitely not at the speed of light. The time-of-relationship (between parent-child and between adults within a community) is slower yet, requiring much repetition, impartiality, sharing, patience and good humor. When we do not take these times into consideration, when we demand that thought and relationship somehow fit into times-of-process that derive from new technologies, then the Heropass (as the comparable times of biological processes) cannot be "reconciled."[14]

It is common today for many people to deny that there is anything significant in the foregoing questions or to deny the significance of the remarkable insights into the nature of our world that have come from quantum and relativity principles. Neither end of that pendulum keeps us in touch with what is real. A more substantive and wholesome *motion* is toward

---

14 Buzzell, *Perspectives*, chapter 1 and *Explorations*, chapters 1 and 11.

a capacity to discriminate—to come to a real, three-brained *measure-of-it*. Somehow, we must climb 'inside' to a viewing place that will permit us to, appropriately and simultaneously, value man's insights into the physical nature of the Universe, respect the powerful but extremely fragile nature of our triune brain and treasure and pursue the *being* values and purposes that have enlivened the heart of the Great Traditions and philosophies.

Gurdjieff's teaching, his wholed manifestation of Work, is a harmoniously integrated vehicle for such an inward-outward journey. It is neither the wisdom of the East nor the science of the West but a remarkable synthesis-in-law of both ~ and more.

THE PRESENT

During the years since the first edition of this text, the penetration of the technological applications of quantum mechanics and relativity theory into the life of the planet has continued to accelerate. In 2007, there are in excess of two and half billion cell phones in use and the life of the Earth is exposed to a trillion times more electromagnetic radiations than life was a hundred and fifty years ago. The biological consequences of these developments are only fragmentarily known. The mobile phone market alone is a multi-billion dollar enterprise. Industry has flooded our world with gadgets—from MP3s, motorized Legos and multimedia systems to iPods, iPhones, Blackberries and Play Stations.

Events taking place ten thousand miles away now influence stock market prices within minutes. Tragedies occurring on the other side of the Earth (over which we have no control) can impact, in minutes, our personal, emotional world and dramatically affect our family relationships. Where mountains and oceans once separated us in time and space, we live in a world of near instantaneous 'times', within 'spaces' that provide little, if any, separation. Our biologically determined triune-brain functions have become, over this ten-year period, even more unable to reconcile these disparities.

This brief text aims to remind and to point. It *reminds* us of our origins some three and a half billion years ago; of the Great Turning which took place with the evolutionary appearance of the first brain and of the successive turnings that evolved the second and third brains. It, thereby, reminds us of our deep and dependent relationship with and on the life-forms that preceded us and with those that accompany us at present. It *points* to a view of human consciousness as a state that builds, in continuity, on previously evolved consciousnesses. In the final chapter, we point to the possibility of personal transformation, via the ~ *intentional digestion* ~ of the images formed by each brain.

FRONTMATTER AND INTRODUCTION PAGE *ii* ENDNOTES
  I Gurdjieff, *Herald of Coming Good*, P 34.
  II Gurdjieff, *Beelzebub's Tales*, P 279.
  III Albert Einstein, *Out of My Later Years*, P 24.

Man—A Three-brained Being

Resonant Aspects of Modern Science and the Gurdjieff Teaching

△ △ △

"... brains in beings serve not only as apparatuses for the transformation of corresponding cosmic substances for the purposes of the Most Great common-cosmic Trogoautoegocrat, but also as the means for beings whereby their conscious self-perfecting is possible."[I]

"This mania began to impose itself upon my being at the time of my youth when I was on the point of attaining responsible age and consisted in what I would now term an 'irrepressible striving' to understand clearly the precise significance, in general, of the life process on earth of all the outward forms of breathing creatures and, in particular, of the aim of human life in the light of this interpretation."[II]

"... I foresaw very soon all the profit it [The Institute for the Harmonious Development of Man] might bring to all humanity, and developed it on a scale to interest and to embrace the entire, so-called, 'sanethinking-world'."[III]

"Wisdom without action hath its seat in the mouth; but by means of action, it becometh fixed in the heart."[IV]

CHAPTER 1
NEW CONCEPTS

Historically, certain ideas about the nature of our world and the nature of life were so revolutionary that their introduction, exploration and verification were marked by extraordinary resistance or marginal acceptance – even as idea or theory. Monotheism, the interdependence of all life, and relativity theory are exemplary of this order of idea. The penetration of these ideas into the emotional and physical life of mankind is a many-centuried process, marked by periods of intense denial, distortion and unbecoming behaviors. A brief glance at the present fragmented and fractious state of our world provides ready confirmation of the difficulties provoked and encountered by such fundamental ideas. Indeed, this order of idea becomes so distorted at times that it may appear to be the source of the resultant conflicts and inevitable suffering and that the solution lies in the eradication of the idea itself. This chapter considers a number of these new concepts.

THE THREE BRAINS

Gurdjieff's introduction of the concept of man as a three-brained being is a fundamental and revolutionary idea. Appearing at a time (circa 1915) when psychology and neurophysiology were in their infancy, when relativity theory had barely been conceived and when warfare had become, for the first time, a whole world phenomenon—the profound significance of the triune nature of man's brain was an enervating principle for a very small number of people for the following thirty-five years.

Man—A Three-brained Being

In the 1950s, Dr. Paul MacLean[1] published the first of many articles which put forward the substrate principle that man had a triune, or three-leveled, brain. MacLean has ably pursued and explored this principle, from a classical evolutionary perspective, up to the present time.

Unfortunately, MacLean's triune brain concept has been, in recent years, substantially set aside by neuroscientists. In part, this is due to the explosive growth of neuroimaging techniques[2] which have captured the imagination of the research community and have focused attention on the participation of various brain modules in a wide variety of chosen events. More fundamentally, the subtlety and evolutionary consistency of MacLean's concept is, as yet, not fully appreciated. When read carefully, his description of the evolutionarily driven "mentations"[3] of the core, limbic and neomammalian 'brains' retains a distinctiveness while, simultaneously, undergoing complex and progressive blendings into what is, in man, a triune cerebral event/process.

The daily life of human beings clearly demonstrates the closely inter-related, but experientially distinct, processes and manifestations of sensation/motion, feeling and thinking. In addition, the processing times of the three mentations are different, their purposes are different and the worlds to which they open (outer, inner and abstract) are distinctly different. Modern psychology, philosophy and all spiritual perspectives will gain in insights when the triune nature of the human brain has been *re*-integrated into modern views.

The physiological, social and scientific implications of a triune-natured brain are so revolutionary that both the people deeply interested in Gurdjieff's teaching as well as those in the current scientific community have largely resisted an impartial exploration, testing and verification of this fundamental concept.

Such evaluation must not remain at a superficial level. Developments in communication (via satellite, TV, fax, computer, etc.), in economic interdependence and in warfare technology have warped and woofed our world into complex, unpredictable and extraordinarily potent (and often malevolent) feedback loops. Each of these developments has become deeply entwined in man's nature as a three-brained being, resulting in disharmonious expressions that formidably threaten the continuity of all life.

Gurdjieff's understanding of this circumstance — of both the lawful, potentially harmonious functioning of the triune brain and of the systematic disharmonies that have led to the present sorrowful situation – was profound. However, he had to speak into the intellectual environment of the early and mid-portion of the 20th century and had to make use of the language and concepts of that time, with all of their relative narrowness of perspective.

---

1 Dr. Paul MacLean (b. 1913 -) coined the expression the "triune brain," to express his perception of the fundamental threeness yet oneness of the human brain, emphasizing, at the same time, the prodigious developmental steps that separate the brain of the reptile from the old and new mammalian brains.
2 e.g., CT scans, MRI, PET scans and functional EEG
3 This term "mentation," denoting a brained process, was chosen independently by both Gurdjieff and MacLean.

Evolution [4]

We posit, for instance, that Gurdjieff was appreciative of the fundamental correctness of Darwin's perspective on biological evolution. What Darwin did not see, however, and what Gurdjieff had to put into a veiled, allegorical form, was that the appearance of brained beings represented a Great Turning in evolutionary history. This turning consisted of the evolution of biological mechanisms (one-brained beings) which could construct sensory images of a resonant portion of the forms and energies of the world external to itself.

The creation, in individuated, sentient forms of life, began to view – to 'see' portions of the Creation itself. Even today, the incredible – truly astonishing – significance of this brained presence within life has not been appreciated. Given the state of knowledge and perspectives of the early 20th century, it would have been even more difficult to appreciate at that time.

Many of the sensation-picturings and the flow of events that occur in the six descents of Beelzebub[5] to the planet Earth are parts of an elaboration on the nature, the relationships between, and functions of the three brains. While often cast in mythic, jocular or seemingly ridiculous and contradictory words and images, these external 'coatings' are actually containers of a series of precise and subtle elucidations of the laws which govern the evolutional unfolding of the three brains (in one-, two- and three-brained forms).

It is also our contention that Gurdjieff speaks from an understanding of the principles that encompass the entirety of life (in its physical, emotional and intellectual aspects). Modern science speaks from a perspective that is focused on the laws of the material world and, historically speaking, has claimed no competence to address the nature of human values and purposes.

Nonetheless, the insights gained by modern science are both remarkable and potentially very helpful in coming to a deeper understanding of Gurdjieff's teaching. In that context, examples of the arenas of potential reconciliation between his teaching and the findings of modern science will be undertaken in this text.

---

[4] Gurdjieff's use of the term "evolution" refers to motion upwards in the Ray of Creation, whereas "involution" refers to motion downward in the Ray of Creation. Darwinian evolution refers to the competitive selection process present throughout the appearance of all life.

[5] See the named chapters in Gurdjieff's *Beelzebub's Tales*.

Gurdjieff's 'Hydrogens'[6]

Gurdjieff approached the classification of matter and energy in a manner remarkably consonant with contemporary scientific views. What they share is the recognition of electromagnetic *bonding* energies as the force that holds various states of matter together. Both views recognize that various orders of em (electromagnetic) forces bind atom to atom and molecule to molecule. Modern chemistry gives these bonds such names as metallic, crystalline, valency, hydrogen, Van der Waals and ionic, whereas Gurdjieff simply selects a type of matter that typifies particular groups of em bonds (e.g., 'iron', 'wood', 'food for man', 'air').

Because the hydrogen atom is the basic building block of the entire atomic table of the elements, Gurdjieff chose to use the term "hydrogen" to refer to the entire range of possible combinations of matter. Ouspensky quotes Gurdjieff, in speaking of "hydrogens," as saying that

"Each of these 'hydrogens' includes a very large group of chemical substances known to us, linked together by some function in connection with our organism."

['hydrogen' 3072 as a piece of 'iron';

'hydrogen' 1536 he defines as 'wood';

'hydrogen' 768 serves as 'food for man';] Further, he says,

"'Hydrogen' 384 will be defined as *water*.

"'Hydrogen' 192 is the air of our atmosphere which we breathe.

"'Hydrogen' 96 is represented by rarefied gases which man cannot breathe, but which play a very important part in his life; and further ... of emanations from the human body, of 'n-rays', hormones, vitamins, and so on; in other words, with 'hydrogen' 96 ends what is called matter or what is regarded as matter by our physics and chemistry. 'Hydrogen' 96 also includes matters that are almost imperceptible to our chemistry or perceptible only by their traces or results, often merely presumed by some and denied by others.

"'Hydrogens' 48, 24, 12 and 6 are matters unknown to physics and chemistry, matters of our psychic and spiritual life on different levels."[7]

These words were spoken around 1915 and reflect the state of knowledge in the chemistry and physics of that time. In fact, they are remarkably prescient, considering the state of knowledge of the digestive process of food during the early part of the 20th century.

Gurdjieff's insights were introduced *prior* to many of the discoveries of science that have greatly extended our knowledge of the "matters of the psychic and spiritual life." Little was known, for instance, about the complex structure of the electron orbitals around atoms or about the different kinds of bonds formed between atoms. The understanding of cations and anions (see glossary)

---

6 The Universe as a continuum of energies, Buzzell, *Perspectives*, "Gurdjieff's 'hydrogens'."
7 P. D. Ouspensky, *In Search of the Miraculous* (San Diego: Harvest/HBJ Book, 2001) pp 174-75. Further references will be noted as *In Search*.

and of electricity was rudimentary, as was the way in which vitamins (the few that had been identified) produce their effects. The neutron would not be discovered for another seventeen years (1932). Likewise, the existence of other galaxies and the expansion of the Universe were not to be known until the late 1920s. There was only a bare suspicion that such energies as the strong and weak nuclear forces even existed.

With respect to the "psychic" matter/energies ($H48$, 24, 12 and 6) which Gurdjieff spoke of as being unknown, it is our conclusion that they are those material/vibrations that are now known to be the functional intermediaries of brained activity.

Viewing the progressive *unbonding* which characterizes the levels of matter, we have come to see and understand H_{3072} ('iron') as crystalline metallic; H_{1536} ('wood') as macromolecular derived from plant life; H_{768} ('food for man') as the class of macromolecular substances (principally with hydrogen bonds), deriving from the tissues of many animals and plants and digestible by humans; H_{384} ('water') as the world of micromolecular liquid; H_{192} ('air') as diatomic molecular; H_{96} ('rarefied gases') as atomic-ionic (+ & -) and H_{48} (the matter/energy substrate of *brained* function) known as ionic-depolarization waves[8] and selective electron transfer. Each of these worlds contains a vast number of possible combinations and relationships and each has proven to be a nearly unplumbable reservoir for research and for the elucidation of various aspects of life processes, including brained functions.

The following table of 'hydrogens', from H_{3072} to H_6, illustrates levels of correspondence with the varied bondings that define each 'hydrogen'.

Levels of 'hydrogen'	Form	Substances	Bonds
3072	macromolecular crystalline minerals & salts	'iron' metals metallic/ionic	metallic interatomic
1536	macromolecular micromolecular (carbon based)	'wood' previously alive – intermolecular	ionic covalent
768	macromolecular micromolecular ionic in solution (active electron-cation-anion exchange)	'food' previously alive, but with resonant molecular forms – (carbon based)	ionic covalent in/out of solution H_2O intermolecular
384	micromolecular molecular-atomic	'water'	covalent ionic (including proton-electron exchanges)
192	molecular-atomic ionic (atmospheric)	'air'	covalent diatomic-ionic (unbonded)

1

---

8 Buzzell, *Perspectives*, see chapter 9, "Gurdjieff's 'hydrogens'," pp 123-25.

Levels of 'hydrogen'	Form	Substances	Bonds
	Interatomic-molecular bonding ends		
96	ionic (atmospheric) — micromolecular with active ionic bonding & proton/electron exchange	rarefied gases vitamins hormones	free ions — cation/anion exchange (including proton & electron)

2

At first glance, there may be confusion about Gurdjieff's inclusion of vitamins and hormones in this rarefied gas level of substances. The confusion is resolved when we recognize that the functional activity of vitamins/hormones resides in the selective, active transfer of cation/anion, or proton/electron. The micromolecular form of the vitamin or hormone is a determinant of appropriate binding or docking sites on the cell membrane. No energy exchange or activation is involved in this alignment process, although it is a major spatial qualifier of the active end of the molecule. Scientific researches have identified many additional substances that function in the same manner including the very important families of enzymes, neuropeptides and neuro-hormones.

At 'hydrogen' 48, we come to the entry level of Gurdjieff's "psychic and spiritual life on different levels." In 1915, almost nothing was known about the interstices of brained function. In the intervening years, a great deal has been clarified regarding the process of neural transmission – at sensory, associative cortical and motor levels.

The nerve impulse itself is known to be a depolarization wave, activated by electron transfers and carried by the rapid, successive movement of positive sodium and potassium ions across the nerve fiber membrane. Given this understanding of neuronal activity (which is the substrate of brained function), the "psychic matters" can be understood in the following way:

Levels of 'hydrogen'	Form	Substances	Bonds (inter-atomic bonds have ceased)
48	depolarization wave forms, dependent on ion transfer	neural impulse – reflexive response	directed depolarization wave (Na-K pump) electron transfer, substrate data for formation of images, activation of complex motor responses
24	intracellular (neural) – orchestrated array of dendritic feedback and modulation	associative neural nets – blending of three brains	creation of micro-electromagnetic fields, the container of images, the beginning of the fusion of these images

3

Note that 'hydrogen' 24 represents the creation of the electromagnetic field – the container of the images associated with each of the brains.

New Concepts

At 'hydrogen' 12, the procreative (or germinative) matter/energy enters. It can also be understood as the first of Gurdjieff's "spiritual" matters. He states that 'hydrogen' 12 corresponds to the element hydrogen of the atomic table. We understand this to infer the capacity to enable the unbonding and creative new bonding of various levels of substances. At the physical body level of procreation, it is the higher force at the essentially solar level of new creation – in the new, hydrogen-bonded linkages of our DNA. It is also this level of 'hydrogen' which can potentially vitalize and vivify the digestion of impressions. One way of compressing the "function ... in the human organism"[9] of this multi-leveled 'hydrogen' would be to say that it has a directable capacity to break old hydrogen bonds and to make new hydrogen bonds. Because it is, simultaneously, the singular proton (as H^+), it carries the clear implication of a solar level resonance with:

~ hydrogen fusion–as the process which creates the atomic table of elements and thus underpins all the possibilities that open into the planetary world (World 24)[10] and,
~ the coalescence of a sun, being lawfully analogous to the coalescence of a singularity (*real* I), thereby becoming a radiant, creative source for its system of planets (or states of *being* and *function*).

Beyond the level of 'hydrogen'12 is 'hydrogen' 6. We understand this as the level which physicists refer to as the carriers of the primordial forces themselves. The photon, as the mass-*less* carrier of the electromagnetic force, mediates (or reconciles) all charged (+ and -) interactions, travels at the speed of light and has frequencies of vibration corresponding to wavelengths from 10^8 to 10^{-16} meters. It is truly a cosmic matter/energy and, at differing frequency ranges, it plays a primordial role in every life-process. The elucidation of photosynthesis and the transformation of photonic energy by our visual system (the archetype of the imaging capacities of the brain) are two of the astonishing and pervasive entries of this level of cosmic matter/energy into life.

We are passive recipients of that energy. What would it imply to be an *active participant* in that infinite range and nuance of energies?

Gurdjieff clearly points to this potential participation, via the functional integration of our three brains, in portions that are part of the full range of matter/energies from 'hydrogen' 48 to 'hydrogen' 6. He speaks of this in a very direct, practical fashion – without recourse to unmeasurable or ultimately mysterious and unknowable energies. While he does emphasize that man, being made in "the image of God,"[11] can participate in resonant *portions* of all levels of the table of 'hydrogens', he does not imply that the full power of the material/vibrations is commensurate with organic life.

9 Ouspensky, *In Search*, p 175.
10 Buzzell, *Perspectives*, see chapter 9, "Gurdjieff's 'hydrogens',"
    and in *Explorations*, chapter 9, "The Power of Symbol."
11 Gurdjieff, *Beelzebub's Tales*, p 775.

Our summary point is that today we stand in a very different place with respect to our knowledge of material/vibrations than humanity did in 1915 or in 1949. Our Work should incorporate this knowledge and appropriately reconcile it with all the other aspects of Work. Most assuredly, Gurdjieff would have done so.

THE UNIVERSE AS MATTER/VIBRATION

It is also possible to view Gurdjieff's table of atoms of the seven Worlds and recognize that the bonding of atoms of the Absolute is the fundamental principle. The matter of each World (from the Absolute down) contains the higher World within it, but is constrained by a particular bonding and, thereby, is held in a denser arrangement; this increasing density progressively limits the allowable motions and decreases its rate of vibration.[12]

An atom of the Absolute ENDLESSNESS	World 1	unification of all forces highest vibratory rate
An atom of 'All Worlds' Protocosmos	World 3	nucleon & radiation (mass-energy)
An atom of 'All Suns' Megalocosmos	World 6	galactic 'cloud' interaction – order of all matter/energy (hydrogen/helium-radiation)
An atom of the Sun Deuterocosmos	World 12	plasma state
An atom of 'All Planets' Tritocosmos	World 24	gaseous (atomic-ionic)
An atom of the Earth	World 48	liquids (water, solutions)
An atom of the Moon	World 96	solids (crystals, minerals metals)

increasing vibration

increasing density

4

---

12 Ouspensky, *In Search*, P 87.

NEW CONCEPTS

All levels below "an atom of the Absolute" can be understood as successive reconciliations of two of the primordial motions:

~ Separation ('away from') and
~ Unification ('toward')

The forces of Separation are coalesced, in the words of modern physics, into the term "temperature" (degrees Kelvin), while the forces of Unification are coalesced in the word "pressure." When we try to conceive of the inconceivable, namely, that state of affairs prior to the Initial Moment, when temperature/pressure are in a perfect state of balance, we are trying to conceive of the state referred to as "Autoegocrat" in *The Tales*. He alludes to the fact that Autoegocrat, as a system, does not work when seen in the context of the "forced need."[13] It is possible to understand this allusion as one of the several ways in which the quantum nature of our Universe is inferred.

Prior to the Emanation, the system of Autoegocrat had been changed to that of Trogoautoegocrat[14] ('I keep myself by feeding'). The initial, outward motions of Separation can be understood as the Emanation from within Holy Sun Absolute.[15] As the initial Separation proceeded, there was a marked decrease in temperature and pressure.

Alternating Separations and Unifications

△ Viewed from the Initial Moment (figure 5a), the forces of Separation (expansion) momentarily become stronger than the forces of Unification (inward pressure).

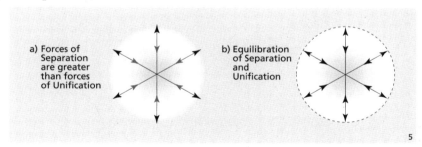

a) Forces of Separation are greater than forces of Unification

b) Equilibration of Separation and Unification

5

△ After a brief interval (5b), the forces of Separation and Unification are brought to a temporary state of balance.

△ With the decrease in the energy of Separation (6c), the state of balance between the two primordial motions is altered. This imbalance is shown in a relative increase in the forces of Unification. A degree of expansion has already occurred, however, and continues by momentum. A different state of balance or reconciliation must be reached, as the original state of unity has been replaced by the rapidly expanding, but still unified, matter/energy field.

---

13 Gurdjieff, *Beelzebub's Tales*, p 748 and Buzzell, *Perspectives*, pp 14-16.
14 Gurdjieff, ibid., discussion of Trogoautoegocrat in particular, pp 750-55 and referenced throughout the book with clues to understanding this most basic principle.
15 Ibid., p 756.

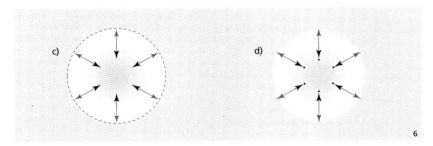

6

△ The forces of Unification (in this instance, the strong nuclear force) become temporarily greater than those of Separation and lead to the first reconciliation (6c and d) which is the containment (confinement) of three quarks[16] and the first appearance of mass (eventually neutron, proton and electron); a Unification of three into one. A third motion appears at this point, a motion *around* or *spin* (not illustrated). The principle of three confined quarks per nucleon holds throughout the three families of massive to least massive quarks (top/bottom, charmed/strange, up/down). As quarks and electrons are considered to be equally primordial, the three singularities of electrons (with muon and tau) and the three singularities of neutrino (with muon and tau) obey the same principle.

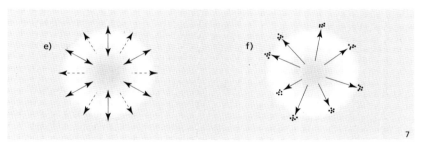

7

△ This first containment encapsulates a large portion of the forces of Unification and leads to a sudden decrease in pressure. This produces another brief state of balance (7e) between the two primordial motions. The initial expansion continues by momentum (7f) and is composed of the products of the first containment plus the high frequencies of radiation deriving from the electroweak force.

△ The initial motion of Separation (Gurdjieff's Emanation from within the Holy Sun Absolute) was not symmetrical. In his elaboration, this asymmetry is a lawful aspect of the changes in the Laws of Three and Seven (both are made "dependent on forces coming from outside"[17] and the Law of Seven has three asymmetries introduced via the interval changes of the third

---

16 Quarks are considered the primordial constituents of protons and neutrons. It takes the combination of three quarks to form a proton or a neutron.
17 Gurdjieff, *Beelzebub's Tales*, p 753.

and seventh Stopinders and the resultant disharmony of the fifth Stopinder). This asymmetry of law becomes of primary importance at the next stage in the creation of the Universe, as it is the fundamental cause of the uneven distribution of matter (protons, electrons, neutrons and helium nuclei). The uneven distribution of expanding matter/energy leads to the gradual coalescence of the great clouds of matter/energy that are to become the galaxies.

△ The coalescence into galactic form is an expression of the primordial motion toward Unification (via the gravitational force) and represents another order of reconciliation (another type of spin or orbital motion). The near infinitude of particleness and radiant energies are drawn into great relational wholes (the galaxies). Within each of them, thousands of millions of stars will gradually form, becoming, in Gurdjieff's words, the "second order suns" or Deuterocosmos (World 12). The expansion of the entire Universe continues, with the separating aspects being the galaxies themselves but not their contents.

The Universe has taken on its fundamental form. It will be a Universe of galaxies (World 6) – each a great whole of its own, bounded by the laws which will underpin the formation and life of the second order singularities (suns). They are second order because they are balanced, singular condensations of matter/energy that recreate higher temperatures and pressures. In a sense, they are analogous to the Holy Sun Absolute but with far less matter/energy and, consequently, return to temperatures/pressures that are only a portion of those present at the Initial Moment. They are also analogous to the Holy Sun Absolute, in that they become creative sources (through their entire lifetime) of the entire atomic table of the elements. This creative expression, along with their wide range of radiated energies, is the potency that underpins the potential appearance of planetary systems, i.e., planets and moons.

△ Continuing the pendulum-like swings between the primordial forces of Separation and Unification, we must look at the coalescence of galaxies and of suns within those galaxies (both are Unifications) and address the Separation which occurs in the time interval between galactic formation and the formation of suns. The ultimate Separation (the continued expansion of the Universe) is entirely the role of the galaxies taken as wholes. They will separate from each other, but their contents will not. It is as if all the remaining initiating force of Separation is placed into galactic motion.

Within each galaxy, there will be a host of relative Separations but all of them will be reconciled within the overall form and sequence of the galaxy itself (the exception being a small portion of light, cosmic rays and neutrinos). The three levels of containment – quark condensation, galactic condensation and solar condensation – bind the Trogoautoegocratic [18] system in motion. Thereafter, all the changes in the Law of Three and the Law of Seven will work themselves out automatically, within the confines of each galaxy.

18 'I keep myself by feeding' is one interpretation of the expression Trogoautoegocrat. This principle interrelates all levels of the Universe and results in the reciprocal feeding (maintenance) of ALL AND EVERYTHING. See Gurdjieff, *Beelzebub's Tales*, pp 130-33.

The working out or manifestation will incorporate:
- △ the spiral movement of the entire galaxy,
- △ the gradual condensation of the first generation of suns (Deuterocosmos),
- △ the elaboration and dispersion of the entire atomic table of elements at the supernova event of many of these first generation suns,
- △ the formation of the second generation of suns (also Deuterocosmos) and, potentially, of solar systems (planets and moons),
- △ the condensations of elements, atoms and their manifold combinations (all of which involve relative Separation and Unification) into what may become terrestrial planets (again depending on a host of relative Separations, such as the orbital distance from the sun and the types of radiant energy) and,
- △ on these terrestrial (solid) planets there is another host of relative Separations and Unifications possible with the potential to produce a mix of solid, liquid and gaseous states of matter which, together, form the primordial substrate for the possible appearance of organic life.

Each of these stages is characterized by a host of relative Separations and Unifications, reconciled by varied and changeable bondings (unifications) that are based on orbitals/rotations and attractions/repulsions (electrostatic, valency and metallic bonds) and which, in turn, are vitalized by physical collision and electromagnetic energy from the sun. Gurdjieff states that all of this, including the possible appearance of life, happens automatically. With the changes in the two primordial Sacred Laws and the Emanation of their forces from within the Holy Sun Absolute, the participation of the Divine Will Power ends.[19]

Thus, from the moment the Universe (and our Time) begins, it is governed by high and immutable law. The motions of Separation ~ Unification, initiated by the Emanation, will carry all the way to the appearance of a brained being (Tetartocosmoses with "independent automatic moving [motion] from one place to another on the surface of the given planets."[20]).

Form and Relativity

As the Creation unfolds, level by level, the successive condensations alternate between interior and exterior forms.

- △ Nucleosynthesis is an interior condensation. Energy is transmuted into mass and encapsulated in singularities – coalescing finally into proton, neutron and electron.
- △ Galactic formation is an exterior condensation. A great mass of individuated particles and associated energies condense into a large scale, unencapsulated form.
- △ Solar formation is an interior condensation. The "previously arisen" (protons, neutrons and electrons – as singularities) are

---

19 Gurdjieff, *Beelzebub's Tales*, p 756.
20 Ibid., p 762.

brought together in an interior condensation, creating (along with supernovae) the entire atomic table of the elements.

△ At the time of a supernova event, the elements created are dispersed into interstellar clouds. This exterior condensation (a grand mix of primordial and newly created nuclear forms) is the substrate for an entirely new generation of stars, with the added possibility of:

~ a relative interior condensation of elements into crystalline atomic forms – minerals, salts, metals, which can gradually coalesce, around the 'new' sun, into a disc of varying densities of matter (an exterior condensation) and,

~ the final interior condensation is into the form of the planets (and moons) themselves.

Each level of condensation reflects the relative participation of one or more of the four fundamental forces, beginning with gravity and progressing through the strong nuclear, weak nuclear and electromagnetic forces. At the level of planets (and life), the forces of gravity and electromagnetism are, by far, the most externally evident determiners of action. However, within these external manifestations of forces, recent scientific research has found and clarified a number of continuing influences exerted by the strong and weak nuclear forces.

THE RAY OF CREATION AND THE MOTIONS OF INVOLUTION AND EVOLUTION

A simple and direct way to understand the terms "involution" and "evolution" is to assign a downward motion to involution (lower temperature/pressure, lower rate of vibration, motion away from World One). Evolution is, then, an upward motion to a higher rate of vibration and higher temperature/pressure ~ a motion toward World One. As a basic principle, this is fine, but the more essential principle of relativity of the manifestations of Creation must also include:

△ The motions, from the Initial Moment of the Emanation to the coalescence of Deuterocosmoses, can all be seen as moving away from the Source and are, therefore, *involutional* (or *downward* in the Ray of Creation).

△ When suns begin to fuse hydrogen and helium, the temperature/pressure (and frequency of vibrations) rises and a motion toward the Source takes place. This is an *evolutional* movement.

△ When planets and moons begin to coalesce — a vast arena of intermolecular and interatomic bondings takes place. These bondings are progressive restrictions in motions, leading down the Ray of Creation and away from the Source – and are therefore *involutional* motions.

△ When atmospheres form around planets like the Earth, (from volcanic action and irradiation from the sun), a portion of the tightly bound minerals and metals are unbound or brought to a less constrained state. This is a far more energetic state, with a higher rate of vibrations than that of solids and is, therefore, an *evolutional* motion.

△ The early atmosphere of the Earth (because of the upward motion of the molten volcanic matter, multiple meteoric impacts and solar radiation) had a temperature of approximately 400° C. This level of temperature induced an interaction, combination and ionization of the matter, thrown up from within the Earth's crust. Enormous quantities of water were one result of these many interactions and, as atmospheric temperature gradually declined (an *involutional* motion), the water condensed from its gaseous state and began to fall to the Earth's surface as rain. It rained torrentially for thousands, perhaps millions, of years. The oceans are the result of that process of condensation. Here, there are fluctuating involutional and evolutional motions.

Triads of Transformation

In this multi-million year event, we are given a beautiful manifestation of the triadic nature of a completed evolutional motion.

All triads of transformation have the same form: 2–1–3

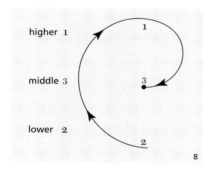

~ a 'lower' (less frequency of vibration, more dense) is acted upon by

~ a 'higher' (higher in frequency of vibration, less dense) and the result is

~ a 'middle' (a blending with density/vibrations between the lower and the higher).

The lower, in the instance of Earth, is the rock (minerals and metals). The higher is the high temperature ash and molten volcanic magma (rising, interestingly, from within the earth and moving upward) which, combined with multiple meteoric impacts and solar radiation, produces the hot, dense atmosphere of the young Earth. From this interaction of higher upon lower emerges the middle – the water environment on the Earth's surface and in its lower atmosphere.

This completed evolutionary triad sets the stage for the emergence of life. The basic motion, which illustrates the application of relativity, is:

~ the interwoven movements of the changed Laws of Three and Seven dictate both upward and downward motions and,
~ if the lower is too dense (and is thereby too resistant to the vibratory level of the higher) or if the higher is not high enough in frequency, then transformation cannot be a result.

In the instance of the triad that produces the watery environment of Earth, there are many dense mineral and metallic substances that strongly resist the higher and, although they are heated to a higher temperature, they return gradually to their crystallized state of 'rockness'. In this instance, the triad is one of interaction (having the triadic form of 1–3–2).[21] Much motion takes place, (i.e., rock may become liquid and radiate much heat) but no internal intermolecular and interatomic bonds are permanently broken and hence no transformation to a higher level of potential occurs.

Gurdjieff calls a state "corresponding"[22] when the higher is high enough and the lower is not too resistant to change. If they are not corresponding, then a triad (or event) other than transformation will unfold.

All transformations in life-forms, including the intentional or conscious transformations possible in Work (which is an accelerated transformation), will demonstrate the same principle of relativity. A completed image of that progressive and resonant process can be found in the five "'being-obligolnian-strivings'."[23] Throughout the exploration of "Man's Triune Brain" (chapter 2, herein), it will be helpful to return to this image.

Conscious Evolution

While the form of the law (2–1–3) and the directions of motion are the same in all triads/octaves of *transformation*, the *conscious* evolution of a human being requires that their three brains actively participate in each step of the process/event. A *something* (we will call it "presence"), must enter the 2, the 1 and the 3. This presence has a distinct and unique quality within each of the three forces of the triad, making possible a succession of choices/decisions that can be reconciled in a unique result – a manifested '3', which is the product of conscious, rather than mechanical events and or processes. Gurdjieff refers to the fundamental enablement of this process as "being-Partkdolg-duty,"[24] with the eventual result being the attainment of the "Reason-of-understanding."[25]

No step in the process of *conscious* evolution will happen by itself, nor can the attainment of a degree of *conscious* evolution by one person be given to another. 'Tastes' may be shared and help through *being*-manifestation can be given ~ but the permanent state is a singularly unique crystallization. There is no spiritual 'Tinker-Bell'.

---

21 These triadic forms are discussed in the appendix in *Perspectives*, by the author.
22 Gurdjieff, *Beelzebub's Tales*, pp 140, 775, 1106.
23 Ibid., p 386 and see the glossary.
24 Ibid., pp 104, 145.
25 Ibid., p 1166.

CHAPTER 1 PAGE 10 ENDNOTES
  I Gurdjieff, *Beelzebub's Tales*, p 144.
  II Gurdjieff, *Herald of Coming Good*, p 13.
  III Ibid., p 40.
  IV Joseph Kimhi, *Schekel Hakodesh*, [no page reference].

"...every such cosmic formation called 'brain' receives its formation from those crystallizations the affirming source for whose arising, according to the sacred Triamazikamno, is one or another of the corresponding holy forces of the fundamental sacred Triamazikamno, localized in the Omnipresent-Okidanokh."[I]

"...these localizations or brains in beings serve not only as apparatuses for the transformation of corresponding cosmic substances for the purposes of the Most Great common-cosmic Trogoautoegocrat, but also as the means for beings whereby their conscious self-perfecting is possible."[II]

"...many people believe that neurobehavioral and neurological observations on animals have little or no human relevance. Standing opposed to such a bias is the evidence that in its evolution, the human brain has developed to its great size while retaining the chemical features and patterns of anatomical organization of the three basic formations characterized as reptilian, paleomammalian and neo-mammalian."[III]

CHAPTER 2
THE TRIUNE BRAIN

INTRODUCTION

The division of life-forms into brained and non-brained beings may be an unfamiliar one to many readers. Classical biology has not used the presence or absence of a central nervous system as a primary means of establishing major categories of life until quite recently. From the early 1970s, with the work of Paul MacLean, Karl Pribram and Wilder Penfield, however, the new and immensely useful division of brained life-forms into first (reptilian or core), second (old mammalian) and third (new mammalian) has become an organizing focus of much productive thought and research.

Dr. MacLean coined the expression, the "triune brain," to express his perception of the fundamental *threeness* yet *oneness* of the human brain, emphasizing, at the same time, the prodigious, developmental steps that separate the brain of the reptile from both the old and new mammalian 'brains'.

This triune division, while new in Western scientific circles, is actually a *re*-presentation of a conception of 'brainedness' that is much older. Gurdjieff set out an exceedingly sophisticated conception of one-, two- and three-brained beings in the early years of the 20th century. It is also important to note that he divided all life-forms into brained and non-brained beings, with the non-brained encompassing microcosmoses (one-celled organisms) and some of the Tetartocosmoses (multi-celled life). He termed all plant life "surplanetary."[1] As we intend to use his primary division of life-forms as our fundamental frame of reference in this chapter, we will set out below a simple comparison of these three perspectives.

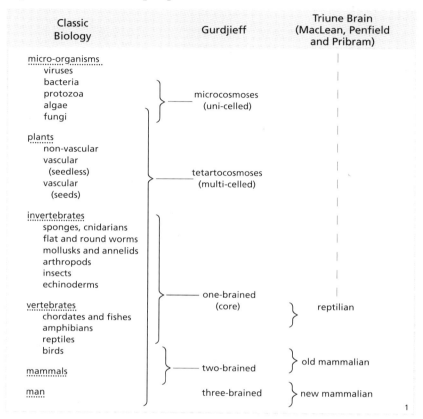

There is a degree of overlap or indeterminacy at the borders of each major group. This reflects the circumstance we encounter in Darwinian evolution when, as we approach a differentiation, there is a blurring of forms and attributes, a "some of this" (old) and "some of that" (new), until we can finally identify and name a clearly defined new life-form.

For example, sponges were long classified as plants because they externally resembled them closely and were fixed or rooted in one place. It took considerable time and many observations to clearly establish that they were, indeed, animals.

The echinoderms, (e.g., starfish), which are amongst the oldest phyla of animals on the earth, have a very primitive neural network that resembles ganglia (a local collection of nerve cells) far more than a brain. However, they have a true endoskeleton and are thus closer, in that respect, to vertebrates

---

1 Gurdjieff, *Beelzebub's Tales*, p 155.

than many of the exoskeletal life-forms (arthropods and insects) with a far more developed brain and sensory-motor system.

A third example and, in many ways the most paradoxical, are the aves (birds). Current evolutionary thought holds that all birds evolved from dinosaurs and/or other early reptiles, as their reproductive cycle via egg laying and exterior embryonic growth is clearly pre-mammalian. Nevertheless, birds share with mammals their endothermy (self-warming) and also their four-chambered heart. They develop and display precise analogs of the social lives of mammals. They are, thus, two-brained life-forms which have evolved from one-brained life but along quite different lines. Even here, there is a blurred edge, as there are flightless birds such as penguins.

With these classification criteria in mind, we can move now to our focal questions, "What is a brain?" and, "What is the triune brain?" and, "Why should a brain have evolved anyhow?"

THE SUCCESS OF LIFE

Life had been present for three billion years and had successfully established itself in an incredible variety of environments. A host of energy/material relationships had been explored and established: thousands of species had differentiated from the primal stock of microcosmoses. The photonic energy of the sun, the atomic-atmospheric energy forms of earth and the melding/binding powers of water had been captured, harnessed and given a self-perpetuating form. Individuation had been assured, the coalescence into multicelled life-forms was well underway and early land plants had established a foothold beyond the tides, bringing the ocean with them, but within. Photosynthesis, the energy storage in ATP, cytoplasmic organelles, complex carbohydrate, fat and protein metabolism, organ differentiation, cell replication and maintenance, independence of an ocean-surround environment – all this was present and thriving. Each step in this emergence of life was an astonishing, astounding accomplishment.

With this degree of success — why would a brain be an evolutionally positive development? Perhaps it is because, in all of this cornucopia of life-expression, there was nothing to see, taste, touch, smell or hear the world beyond the cell membrane. In all of life, up to this point, there had been no instrument capable of building images and moving itself on and into the world beyond itself. Life was blind, deaf and lacked autonomous movement. While enormously vibrant, exploratory and successful, it was unable, in any way, to be *aware*, either of itself (as being alive and individuated) or of the vast panoply of forms, shapes, colors and motions beyond its bodily surface. The microscopic forerunners of the senses were atomic-molecular-strivings-to-blend or electromagnetic attractions/rejections of molecular forms. No image of a whole, outside of itself, was possible.

Yet, we reiterate our question, "Why should there be a brain?" The life that had appeared on earth was richly diversified, having established itself securely, in a wide variety of hostile environments — even without the appearance of external senses and a central integrative network that could initiate and control movement. Think of the pressures existing at the bottom of five miles of ocean or the temperatures near volcanoes, within glaciers and on deserts. For over three billion years, we could say that life had strongly affirmed its presence and, via its persistence and diversification, demonstrated its objective faith (its capacity to be: to persist and to remain fundamentally what it is).[2]

However, where, in all this microcosmic and multicelled life, is there a sense of the future? What is ten, one hundred or even a thousand years when there is no individuated, subjective experience of time; when the 'future' does not exist, even in potential form, until it is the 'present'?

All of life, up to this juncture, was pinioned upon surface interactions (the external cell membrane in microcosmoses and the boundary cell layer in multicelled forms). The world *out there* was what presented itself directly to the external boundary of the life-form. Food was not around the corner or under that rock; it did or did not appear at the boundary membrane. Truly, then, spontaneity was present in every moment and, therefore, no different from any other moment because it could not be otherwise. Time, for non-sentient life, was and is, wholly collapsed into or focused upon the *present* moment. Only a millimeter's distance away from the surface membrane there *may* lay a source of food. For that membrane, this is beyond the present moment in a strange dimension that collapses both time (a possible future event) and space (an unmeasured and immeasurable distance). The source of food does not *exist* until direct contact is made with the surface membrane. By direct contact, we mean to include any carrier of information – be it in molecular or ionic form or an electromagnetic radiation. Each of these is certainly a carrier of information that can produce reactions at the cell membrane level but they are not yet *images* of the outside world. There is no process of the transformation of energies at the cell boundary that will serve to reconstruct a whole image of something in the outside world. Rather, the molecular, ionic and photonic energies are *initiators* of a single or a chain reaction that begins at the cell surface in that moment.

Uni- and multicelled organisms, therefore, live in their *present* moment, within times and spaces that are beyond their knowing. Its faith-in-itself is unquestionable, supported by a constancy and persistence of life that stretches through a past of three billion years.

Why a Brain?

With this context in mind, we may ask more specifically, "What can a brain bring to this remarkable affirmation/constancy of life?"

It can bring hope. Why hope? Because, the objective essence of hope lies in the confident, exploratory motion, built on *faith* ~ which can engage in a perceived but undetermined future.[3]

---

2 Buzzell, *Explorations*, chapter 7, "The Cosmic Dimensions of Faith, Hope and Love."
3 Ibid., pp 108-11.

The Triune Brain

For that to appear, life must reach into this perceivable future. It does that by creating resonant images of the world beyond its boundary layer and it must be able to move into and actively explore that world. Without a self-moving capacity, the ability to image the world would serve no *wholing* purpose. By "wholing," we refer to the process of coming to an organized *one* or singularity.[4] Moreover, without survival or persistence in form, whether measured by food, defense or mating, there could be no experiential exploring. Survival becomes, for an emerging first-brain creature, the primal reconciling force, balancing each developing ability to image the world with a resonant capacity in motion.

The first brain will build or create these resonant images from octaves of photonic, atomic and molecular forms, motions and energies (figure 2a) and the triadic form of afferent inputs, image-building and organized, patterned reactions (2b). The efferent motor expression of the pattern will have its individuated *reconciling* impulse necessarily built around survival. Survival itself is triadic: to survive 1) by finding/taking in food, 2) by defending itself/escaping a predator, and 3) by finding a mate/reproducing itself (figure 2c). Survival, or persistence-in-form, thus relates the one-brained creature to the present moment, the near future and the distant future.

The fully evolved first brain adds an infinitude of dimensions to life. Commensurate with the exploration and gradual development of the external senses, comes an equally commensurate exploration and enhancement of the moving-center capability.[5] Even controlled motion through the air (flight) is added to the controlled motions within the liquid ocean and on/in the dry land surfaces (2d).

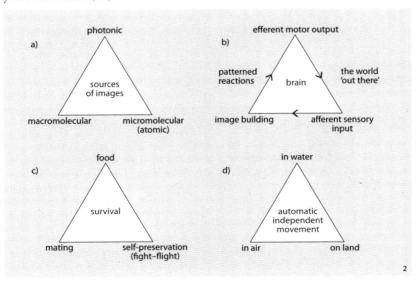

2

---

4 David Bohm, *Wholeness and the Implicate Order*, (London: Routledge, 1980), Introduction and chapter 1 and Buzzell, *Explorations*, "Gurdjieff's Creation Myth," pp 194-97.
5 Gurdjieff, *Beelzebub's Tales*, p 762.

Most modern biologists consider the age of the dinosaurs as the pinnacle of development of the first brain. Looking at the diversity, sophistication and successful survival (200 million years) of this acme of one-brained beings can evoke a sense of wonder and humble respect for the quite incredible capacities of such a brain. It is, equally, a dramatic statement of the interstices (however automatic) of hope.

With all its subtleties and power, however, the first brain could only see (and hear, taste, touch and smell) into the outside world. The *inside* world, the world within its own body, remained essentially *un-imaged*.

While the control of all bodily functions (from digestion and repair to energy storage and musculoskeletal coordination) undergoes a parallel refinement and expression throughout the history of one-brained beings, an afferent or inner sensory system capable of building images of that inside world does not appear.

For this, a much higher level of energy production will be necessary and to accomplish this, many new organs and refinements of established organs must take place. This inner sensory system, with equally sophisticated inner-world imaging and inner motion control, emerges with the second brain.

IMAGES

image [L. imaginem, acc. of imago, imitation, copy, image < base of imitari, to imitate] 1. the optical counterpart of an object, each of whose points acts as a source of light which is reflected in a mirror or focused by a lens. 2. a thing resembling another thing, a likeness.[6]

Images are likenesses; resonant representations of some aspect of the world inside or the world beyond the external membrane of a creature.

Proportionality or ratio is the basis of its resonance. Of the eighty some octaves in the spectrum of electromagnetic (photon) radiation, visible light encompasses slightly less than one full octave (4000 to 7000 angströms). Electromagnetic waves, of wavelength 4000 angströms (angström $A = 10^{-8}$ cm), are experienced in human vision as the color violet. Similarly, wavelengths of 7000 angströms will be experienced as the color red: 4000 angströms is to violet as 7000 angströms is to red. Our sun's surface radiates across a large portion of the electromagnetic spectrum, with a peak wavelength at what humans experience as green-yellow light. The specialized cells of the human retina (cone cells) are responsive to the electromagnetic waves (4000 to 7000 angströms) proportional to their density.

Neural impulses, which are generated from the multiple layers of retinal cells, travel to the back of the brain (the occipital lobe to the visual cortex). The area of the distribution and intensity of impulses is proportionate to the number of cone cells stimulated by the different wavelengths of visible light. This resonance between different light wavelengths and cone cell sensitivities forms the basis for a color image.

6 *Funk and Wagnalls Standard College Dictionary*

The Triune Brain

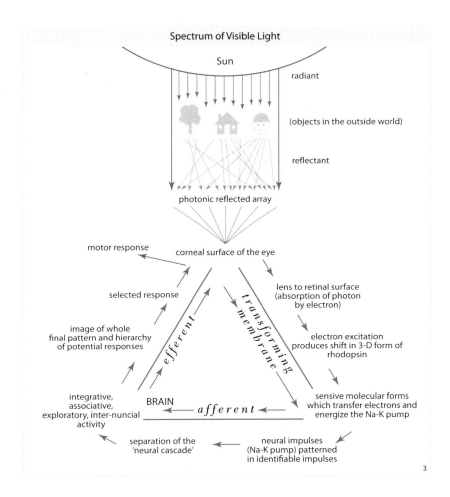

The Electromagnetic Spectrum

The resultant color image is a proportional representation of the type, intensity and distribution of visible light waves (photons) entering the eye. This image is a miniature *whole*, a likeness deriving ultimately from the visible spectrum but modified by the varying absorption/reflection of photons by the outside world.

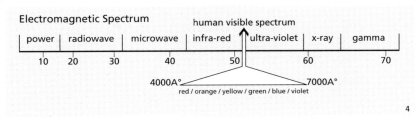

In one-brained creatures, we can trace a very long and slow development of the external senses and the motion instruments. This begins as early as the non-brained, one-celled flagellate, Euglena (with microscopic eyespots which, although light-sensitive, are not truly productive of an image) and extends to Copilia (the smallest one-brained creature capable of forming true images with primitive lenses, retinas, optic nerves and a microscopic brain).

Throughout this period of lavish and prolonged experimentation, the visual sense becomes located in remarkable places – on stalks, antennae, joints and body protrusions of great variety. Multiple eyes, serving near and distant vision, are also found in one-brained creatures. Additionally, the wavelengths of electromagnetic radiation, which form the image-building potential, extend beyond a human's visible spectrum. Many varieties of insects have visual systems sensitive to infrared wavelengths while others register and form images in ultraviolet wavelengths.

While we find visual imaging systems of great variety, sensitivity and sophistication in one-brained creatures, the common attribute we wish to emphasize is the emergence of the capacity to image the world *outside* in resonant representation, utilizing a portion of the photonic energy of the sun.

The building of images of the world beyond the boundary membrane of living creatures is not limited to visual systems. The first brain was engaged from the outset in parallel image-building efforts that opened into the vibratory and atmospheric world of sound waves, the molecular world of taste and smell and the macromolecular (solid and vibrating) world of the tactile (touches).

We began our exploration of *image* with the eye because it is a prime achievement of sensory evolution and we ordinarily associate images with vision. Therefore, it seemed more appropriate to use the visual system as a model for this resonant representation. The imaging *process* and the resultant *event* will be analogous with each of the other senses.

Images in Sound

In remarkably analogous fashion to the octavic spectrum of electromagnetic waves, there is an octavic spectrum in sound waves. Fundamentally, sound is a compression-rarefaction wave transmitted through the molecular world (of solids, liquids and gases), initiated by a sudden mechanical disturbance or distortion of the elastic relationships of the molecular world. We put it in these defining terms not just to be scientifically correct but, since sound is both pervasive and profoundly significant in the world of three-brained beings, it is most essential to identify both its origin and nature. In addition, sound, especially in its lower frequencies, melds into the world of macromolecular vibration and is thus intimately related to the tactile (many *touches*[7]) senses.

The human auditory spectrum extends from sound waves of 15 cycles per second (CPS) to approximately 20,000 CPS (a bit over 10 octaves). Some young children are known to register recognition up to 30,000 CPS and many older

---

7 There are multiple touch receptors: light touch, deep touch, stretch, heat and pain.

persons cannot register much beyond 4,000 CPS (the highest note on a piano). Other life-forms, analogous to the varying sensitivities of life's visual systems, register well below 15 CPS, (i.e., worms and fish) and above 30,000 cycles CPS. The ultrasonic range of bats extends, at least, to 80,000 CPS. In that range, there is much evidence that a bat's brain forms a whole image – much like a visual image, akin to the ultrasonic imaging techniques now being used in diagnostic medicine and industry.

The auditory sense is closely related to balance and position. In early one-brained creatures (ocean), the predecessor of the gas bladder (used by fish to balance themselves within the totally fluid medium) made use of a tiny pebble which, rolling from side to side within the bladder, stimulated hair-like fibers which sent impulses to a primitive brain. These impulses served to orient the creature (vertical/horizontal) and were linked to motor/muscle contractions. This simple principle evolved, as the bladder wall could also vibrate in response to sound waves, into the organ of Corti, the sensitive heart of the human cochlea.

It is now understood that the membrane apparatus transforming sound waves into neural impulses (analogous to the retinal apparatus for vision), operate on the piezoelectric principle. This principle is based on the phenomenon that mechanical deformation of certain ionic crystals will induce an electric current. The mechanical deformation in the hearing system would be initiated by the vibration of the eardrum and the direct transfer, via the bony ossicles, to fluid waveforms in the cochlea. There, the fluid waves set tiny hairs into resonant vibration, deforming crystals at the base of the hairs and inducing a tiny electric current. Above a certain threshold these tiny currents trigger a nerve impulse to the auditory cortex.

Aural images in the early first brain were largely concerned with spatial orientation (both balance in space and location), relative to other life-forms and objects. The remarkable coherence of schools of fish and other ocean creatures is based on this form of image. Over time, additional images are formed which are largely messages; warning signals of prey/predator and alerting signals of possible mates.

The sound waveforms, extending over time and containing variable combinations of frequencies, became highly individualized, encoded messages with specific, compressed meanings. As the afferent (input) hearing apparatus gained in sophistication, moving-center capacities also evolved the ability to generate specific sounds, which are linked by muscular or efferent (output) responses to the *meaning* that is inherent in the messages. Truly, they are the first-brain forbearers of human speech and word recognition. We can also recognize archaic musical forms of communication and hearing in the chirping, clicking and buzzing sounds of insects and their motor response in dance and other formalized movement patterns aligned with mating rituals.

Our essential emphasis here, as with the visual sense, is on the analogous, resonant representations of the world outside and the building of images from sound waves that the first brain explores and develops.

Images of Taste and Smell

We enter the world of three-dimensional (stereotactic) molecular forms with the senses of taste and smell. Our present understanding of the transformation of smell and taste into resonant nerve impulses is based on a modified lock-key mechanism found on the surface of the olfactory and taste cells. Molecules that are volatile (evaporating into the air and being drawn into the nose) go into solution in the mucous overlying the cells of the olfactory bulb. Their three-dimensional form ~ the key ~ is potentially aligned to one or more of seven molecular depression/projections ~ the lock ~ on the cell membrane. A fit between the molecule and the receptor site activates an electron transfer process within the cell, increasing its potential for neural discharge.

A nerve impulse results when enough molecules of a specific type have activated enough locks. As few as eight molecules of a substance will trigger a single nerve impulse (in humans) and forty nerves must be stimulated before we can identify a smell.

To give an appropriate sense of proportion and sensitivity, we must have in mind that the olfactory (smell) apparatus in humans has approximately seven million cells. Science has identified seven primary molecules of smell, each distinctive in three-dimensional shape and electric charge, and each with a complimentary cavity having projections and electric charges on the cell membrane.

In the instance of taste, the situation is similar but generally less sensitive. In humans, for instance, it takes 25,000 times as many molecules to elicit a specific taste and there are only four classes (sweet, bitter, salty and sour), each having quite widely separated sites of taste cells within the mouth. This decrease in sensitivity appears to be because taste deals with molecules in liquid and solid form rather than in the gaseous state.

As the first brain developed and these senses of taste and smell differentiated, the images formed are analogs of the world outside. Other life-forms, sources of food, toxic substances and potential matter can become identified through their molecular, geometric correspondences. Great areas and long distances (miles for certain insects) are scanned by the sense of smell and a remarkably reliable picture of the important contents of that space is reconstructed by the first brain. Taste, requiring more direct contact with the solid and liquid states of the outside world, seems reserved to imaging wholes – as food, potential toxins or final identification of a mate.

With the coming of the second brain, the acute sensitivity of smell and the parallel capacity of the brain to image the contents of the atmospheric world will develop into a unique and multi-potent sense. The olfactory cell has a self-regenerative ability and an exclusive afferent/input channel to the second brain. This direct channeling of input forms the substrate for the powerful emotional responses and clear memory images characteristic of the second brain.

Tactile Images

Imagine that you have been asked to close your eyes and an object about the size of a tennis ball is placed in your hand. You are then asked to report everything you can about this object.

You feel its weight in the palm of your hand. It is slightly cooler to the touch than is your own hand-to-hand contact and its surface, while smooth, is not slick. It is rounded but a little eccentric, having a low-pitched bumpy ridge that extends about a quarter of the circumference. A small, sharp edged pit, perhaps an eighth of an inch across, lies midway just to the side of the ridge. Squeezing it gently, you report that it yields a little, regaining its shape instantly when you release the squeeze. The ridge you identified earlier is more firm, resisting your gentle and, then, firmer pressure. You shake it gently and feel a slight vibration that seems to come from a subsurface region. You conclude from several shakings that there is a layer of something forming the outer covering, perhaps a 1/4 inch thick and that the interior is mobile, perhaps liquid. You have formed a three-dimensional image—through 'touchings'.

Subtleties of Touch

Because the macromolecular world contains such a variety of identifiable characteristics, imaging this world requires a number of quite distinct transformer/receptors.

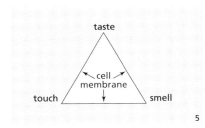

5

Touch is often referred to as the ancient or first sense. It makes use of the principle of molecular contact/touching that took place between the cell membrane of early microcosmoses and the multitude of the protein and sugar-like molecules dissolved in the surrounding ocean. Nevertheless, this is also the germinal circumstance for taste and smell, so perhaps it would be more accurate to say that all three 'molecular' senses share the same primordial contact.

Touch, like taste, appears to have four major categories of transformer/receptors – pressure, hot, cold and pain. Life, especially of the two- and three-brained variety, has differentiated these four categories with such subtle and interwoven nuances that an infinitude of subjective experiencings has resulted. For example, recall the distinctive qualities of a pat, a lick, a scratch, a pinch, a hug, a nudge, an itch, a prick, a tingle, a tearing/lacerating pain, the coolness/contact of an ice cube or the precise hot pain of a drop of lead solder.

While the touching senses do not develop this degree of sophistication in one-brained beings, they do undergo progressive differentiation into powerful tools that dimensionalize and whole the outside, macromolecular world. Lacking hair, soft skin and the energy capacity to be self-warming, their discrimination of heat, cold and surface pain has limited expression.

What does develop with remarkable precision is the ability to image, by touch, the three-dimensional qualities of the macromolecular world, both at rest and in motions that directly affect the organism. Moreover, since touch is an overall bodily sensation (reflecting the entire cell membrane responsiveness of a microcosmos), there will be a *dual* exploration and development of this sense. One aspect remains diffused over the body surface, serving as a three-dimensional guide and/or warning system (in crawling, tunneling, fighting, mating). The other aspect is focused on highly specialized body parts (antennae, wings, limbs, head) which concentrate and refine the touches and their central brain connections into tools that image the three-dimensional world surrounding the creature. Here, we find many examples of the close relationship that develops between the motor (efferent or response) aspect of the brain and the sensory (afferent or input) aspect of the brain, often residing within the same body part.

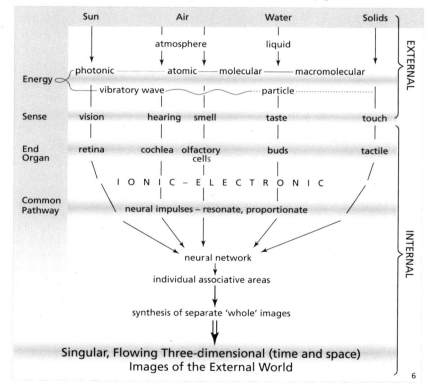

Blendings of the Senses

Our brief exploration of the senses may create an inaccurate impression of their separateness. In actuality, all of the senses underwent a simultaneous and closely interwoven development. The images of the three-dimensional world derived from touch are simultaneously melded with those of smell, taste, hearing and vision. For the individual life-form, the relative times and motions of each sense are reconciled into an experiential process that becomes a consistent and resonant whole.

Awareness, through the multidimensional windows of the first brain, enters, explores and refines tools of perception and builds more and more complex wholes of the world beyond the external membrane of the life-form. This incredible feat is accomplished by bringing four levels or worlds[8] into a real and flowing relationship with each other.

The following illustration gives a form to the essential aspects of the relationships and blendings discussed.

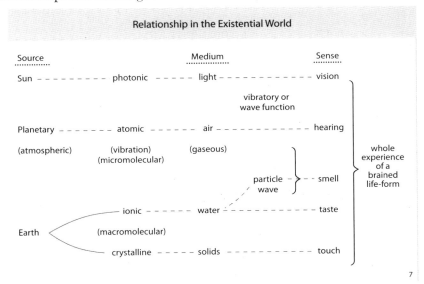

Processing of Visible Light

Research in molecular biology has begun to penetrate this world of the transformative membranes of the senses and a host of astonishing, exciting events have been imaged for the first time. We use the word "image" in precisely the same sense as we have throughout this chapter. The imaging instruments used to peer into the electronic-ionic-molecular world are called pump-probe lasers that can empower stroboscopic snapshots in time intervals of femto-seconds (0.000000000000001 sec. or 10^{-15} sec.). The initial process of photon absorption and internal rearrangement of the three-dimensional form of the rhodopsin (light sensitive) molecule takes 200 femtoseconds (200×10^{-15} sec.).

A relative notion of this processive time interval can be hinted at if we were to ask how many of these events would occur in one second, given that

---

8 those levels or worlds being photonic, electronic, atomic and molecular

each molecular rearrangement were immediately followed by another. The answer is 5,000,000,000,000 (five trillion). Alternatively, the proportion could be put in terms of a daily event like brushing your teeth. If you spend two minutes brushing your teeth (a short process) and we make this equal to the 200 femtoseconds interval, for how long would you brush your teeth, in two-minute cycles, to make it equivalent to one second of femto-time? ... approximately 19 billion years!

This little example is intended to show how incommensurate the times of photonic-molecular events and our daily experience of events appear to be. It is miraculous that, via the reconciling power of life, these times are brought into a relationship; one that harmoniously links these vastly separate worlds.

THE SECOND BRAIN (INCLUDING THE LIMBIC SYSTEM, CINGULATE GYRUS, HYPOTHALAMUS AND AMYGDALA)

The second or emotional brain has its material base in the same worlds as the first brain. The emerging uniqueness of the second brain is its capacity to *image* and to move the world *inside* the boundary membrane (the skin surface) of the life-form. For this to happen, an enormous increase of energies is required.[9] The biological sciences have explored in considerable depth the adaptations and new developments that provide the increase in energy resources and the instruments (organs, tissues, chemical processes) which organize their expression. Thus, we see the emergence of those external distinguishing features of mammalian life-forms: a four-chambered heart, diaphragm, uterus, mammary glands and a self-warming capacity.

This remarkable increase in the quality and quantity of higher energies (mostly atomic, electronic, ionic) makes possible the interpenetration of the first brain by the second and the development of an entire arena of inner senses, complemented by a kaleidoscope of molecular forms that serve as messenger indicators of the spectrum of evoked emotional states. The resultant images and the inner-moving expression of them, when illuminated by the expanding *awareness* at the core of the second brain, produces the *sense-of-self* which is so clearly recognizable in mammalian life.

We recognize the exterior reflection of this sense-of-self modulated by inner and outer events and, from moment to moment, in the subtle (and often not so subtle) diversity of facial expressions, gestures, postures, carriage and tones of voice. These become, as mammalian life evolves, an extremely versatile and essential *language*, communicating a sense-of-self powerfully and specifically into the social, interactive and personal life of two- and three-brained beings.

The reality and potency of this sense-of-self is in no wise diminished by referring to it as the result of a causal/determined process. While the second brain opens to an arena of awareness infinitely beyond the external awareness inherent in the first brain, it is bounded by its subjectivity. It is not aware of itself and *simultaneously* aware that it is experiencing fear or anger but is

---

9 of oxygenated blood, glucose, proteins, fats, enzymes, nerve and muscle control

within or has become the state of fear or anger, with no sense-of-itself as separate from the particular state. It is only when the third brain is well along in its development (coating), that a separation is possible which brings a fuller awareness of itself, quite apart from the changing emotional and/or physical states.

The Inner Senses
Many of you likely have already asked, "What are these inner senses? If they exist, then why are they not described in the same straightforward manner as the external senses?"

Partly, this seems due to the history of the Western biological sciences. There has always been a strong tendency in modern science to observe the world from a structural/functional perspective and to emphasize quantitative, descriptive aspects of any phenomenon. Qualitative differences are not a starting point for the vast majority of Western-trained scientists. The real leaps forward have been made by such minds as Newton, Semmelweis, Darwin, Planck, Heisenberg and Einstein who ask qualitative as well as quantitative questions. A large majority of scientists quantitatively elaborate on the insights made by very few.

For many years the development of the brain was viewed largely from this perspective. The brain grew larger and more complex, with new bodily organs and functions appearing that required careful structural study and analyses. In qualitative terms, the uniqueness of the second brain has only recently begun to be recognized. Even more important for our line of exploration in this chapter is the qualitative uniqueness of the third brain. In this, we feel there is substantial evidence that what Western man has identified as the distinguishing features of the third brain, (i.e., the capacity for logical, processive thought, language, mathematical skills, invention and art) is only the tip of the iceberg. In large part, it is limited to the functional 'obviousnesses' of human capacity and expression.

It is also, in part, because most humans function from a second-brain awareness nearly all of the time. It is a relatively rare event, when we stand within the third brain, able to use the powers of the second and first brains, with a degree of impartiality. The vast majority of the time, we are influenced by the automatic consequences of the functioning of the first two brains. The result is that we are immersed in the images produced by the inner senses and have great difficulty in coming to an awareness of them as sensory-motor instruments rather than as the sense-of-self and the consequential feeling of 'I' which is so strongly attached to it.

An example from everyday life may help to make these points of differentiation more clear. We all could see ourselves become irritable and/or defensive because of a phone call from the bank or a tense conversation with one of our children. In that moment, we *are* that mood or state, as is pointed out to us when our spouse or a friend enters the room and, without any words from us, asks, "What's the matter – you look upset?" Our facial expression and posture have, in a brief moment, communicated a very clear impression. Our inner state is being reflected in the interpenetration of the first brain (our musculoskeletal apparatus) by the second brain. The functional *moving center* of the second brain is, in part, the sophisticated gamma or muscle spindle system. The central origins of this monitoring/modulating system is intimately tied to the limbic system, (i.e., the hippocampus, cingulate gyrus, amygdala and hypothalamus), the core of the second brain. Our emotional state of the moment has, thus, a direct route of subtle expression through the modulation of the muscles of facial expression, gesture, carriage and posture. This image is seen by our spouse or friend and leads to their question.

Yet, are we *aware* ourselves – in that moment, of the raw expression which is on our faces – of the furrows in our forehead, the down-turned lines of our mouth, the tightness of the muscles around our eyes or the too-rapid, choppy gesture of the hand? When we speak, are we aware of the higher pitch and diminished resonance of our voice? Each of these manifestations is an efferent expression of the state defined by the present activity of the second brain. Our sense-of-self, in that moment, is the causal, subjective experience of the interior 'climate'. Therefore, often we find that this resultant state is a major determiner of the sense-of-self that moves into the next event. To continue the example, let us suppose that our prior conversation with our child is only one of many unsatisfactory conversations and that we are reluctant to admit to our spouse that we have, once again, come away from an interaction without a balanced resolution. So we say, "I'm alright – why do you always think something's wrong?" and we say it with such a bite! Nevertheless, our second brain-modulated expression has given us away and, by denying it, we have simply added another deceit to our list of unreal, un*whole*some behaviors.

From this ordinary life example, it is possible to see that at least part of the incoming data that feeds into the second brain via the inner senses has to do with a remarkable capacity to image and give meaning to forms and patterns of motion. Raw data enters via the external visual sense (first brain) but the resultant image is scanned by the second brain and a subtler and far more refined image of meanings is formed. For the second brain, meanings always appear to concern some aspect of social or interpersonal life and how the sense-of-self is confirmed, denied, recognized and supported, or challenged and moved toward conflict.

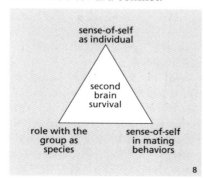

8

This is analogous to the meanings given to the images in one-brained creatures. There, we noted that 1) physical survival in the moment, 2) survival by identifying and taking in food and 3) survival into the distant future by finding a mate and reproducing, are the elements in the triad of the first brain. Second-brain survival can still be seen as the reconciling core of its triad but now survival concerns the inner sense-of-self.

A graphic example of this can be seen in the wide spectrum of interactive events that take place among the members of a colony of apes. Jane Goodall's twenty-year observations amply illustrate the essentiality of gesture, posture, facial expression and a variety of grunts and screeches (tone of voice) in the social heirarchizing and interpersonal life of this advanced two-brained being. The sensation-picturings created by Gurdjieff in Beelzebub's fourth descent[10] (when he considers the origin of the apes) have a powerful resonance with this perspective on the second brain.

We can also recognize the penetrating subtlety of the second brain with the refinements that take place in the sense of hearing. We alluded to an aspect of this when we included tone of voice in our ordinary-life example. The *inner octaves* often mentioned in Work are exemplified here. The second brain has the capacity to hear *into* sounds to a degree infinitely beyond the first brain. We have only to recall the tonal qualities in our father's voice when he spoke our name in endearment (on Christmas morning), in question (as in, "Where are the keys to the car?"), or in anger (as when we conveniently forgot our chores). In each case, and in many others we can individually recall, there is an image-in-sound of the inner meaning that goes far beyond the word itself and is contained in the inner resonances and overtones of the voice.

The sense of smell underwent an especially dramatic imaging transformation with the coming of the second brain. With 270 million smell receptor cells (compared to our 7 million), the imaging capacity of the wolf is far beyond our comprehension. The wolf lives in an 'ocean' of smell, with images flowing in great abundance, informing it not only about what other creatures have been here, but when, from what direction, their size and age, their species and much about their state. Adding to its significance is the fact that only the sense of smell has 1) direct route to the second brain, bypassing the processing centers in the thalamus that all other senses go through and 2) cells that retain their ability to regenerate throughout life, unlike most other nerve cells.

Smell, via the second brain, opens the inner octaves of this sense by developing a remarkable sensitivity to the hormonal and other volatile secretions/excretions of other creatures. The emotions of fear, anger, rage and the states of sexual responsiveness and age are only a few of the inner octaves of the molecular world that are dense with specific and elaborate meaning, adding an important dimension to the visual and auditory images.

With the development of soft skin and hair, touch undergoes perhaps the broadest imaging development with the second brain. The capacity to self-warm is dependent on receiving, from the skin surface, accurate data regarding contact temperatures (of air, objects, other creatures) and the sophistication of these temperature-sensitive, afferent receptors (for both hot and cold) becomes astonishing. Equally astonishing is the sensitivity of touch that appears with hair; a displacement of 0.00004 inch of a downy hair being sufficient to initiate a nerve impulse.

---

10 Gurdjieff, *Beelzebub's Tales*, p 268 and further.

Touch is so ubiquitous and extends over such a wide range of applications, that cessation of excitability has been built into it. After a period of responsiveness, the superficial and deep touch receptors cease to report until a change in touch occurs.

Pain registration undergoes equally impressive diversification and spatial specificity within the second brain. Additionally, the second-brain pain of the loss of a mate, offspring and social position becomes overtly evident in the changes of posture, vocal and facial expression and physical behavior. Its personal, subjective meaning is as real and elaborate, both individually and collectively, to a family of monkeys or a colony of apes, as it is to humans. To watch a mother cat lick her young, two giraffes rubbing each other's necks or young porpoises touching, nudging their mother and being touched in return gives us hints as to shades of emotional meanings (the inner octaves) carried by the afferent and efferent limbs of the sense of touch.

Recent research has emphasized the variety of touches in the normal growth and development of all (including human) mammalian life-forms. Physical growth, cellular development of the nervous system itself and the powerful social and emotional sense-of-belonging, of being in a valued relationship – all are potently influenced by touches appropriately repeated in the very young. The emotional or touch messages to the giver and receiver have been demonstrated to be critical to the normal personal/social life of all animals investigated. Lacking this tactile/relational expression, the young of many species never develop normally, either physically or in their ability to fit into an appropriate social role in the den, colony or family, even if touching is resumed or promoted at later stages.

This brief excursion into the penetration of the first brain's external senses by the second brain and the further digestion of these senses to the level of emotional (self-other) meanings and concerns, as we have alluded to before, only that portion of the inner senses directly tied to the outer world. The second brain also elaborates a new group of afferent receptors and efferent motor instruments[11] that interpenetrate the internal organs and tissues and become the sources of wholly new types of images and central response patterns. We will briefly focus on two of them: the gamma or muscle spindle system and the sympathetic/parasympathetic (autonomic) nervous system.

The Gamma System

We have made mention earlier of the role of muscle spindles in the minute motor control of the muscles of facial expression, gesture, posture and tone of voice. To illustrate the delicacy of control contained in this system, we need only refer to the comparative densities of spindles in the facial and hand muscles (250 per gram of tissue) and the large spinal erector muscles (15 per gram of tissue). The high density of spindles permits an extremely refined and rapidly adapting system of responses of tiny portions of each of the muscles of

---

11 Buzzell, *Explorations*, chapter 2 "The Emergence of the Function of Emotion," p 18.

the face and hands. In microseconds, the resting tone and the number of responding groups of muscle fibers can be altered over a very large range. This level of modulation is what makes it possible for the hand to become the delicate motor instrument of a watchmaker, sculptor or surgeon or the immensely strong applied force by a lumberjack or coal miner. The gentle stroke of a mother's fingers (with a controlled application down to thousandths of a gram) or of a lover's caress become possible only through the patterned or imaged expression which has its origin in the second brain but flows outward and finally beyond the body via the reconciling instrument of the *spindled* musculoskeletal motor system. Simultaneously, the muscle spindle system becomes the instrument of expression of the emotional life, transforming the self-image within into the personality masks which are worn by the face and hands. Even the total body posture comes under the refining influence of the spindle. While large skeletal muscles make it possible to hold and move the bony levers of the spine and extremities in semi-upright, crawling and running positions, the deep, short muscles (spanning only one or two spinal/vertebral segments) finely modulate and adjust balance, posture and carriage. These deep, short muscles have a density of spindles close to that of the face and hands and are interwoven into the overall function of the cerebellum.

It has been less than twenty years since sympathetic nerve fibers have been demonstrated to directly innervate muscle spindles. This long assumed and now corroborated linkage establishes a beautiful relationship among the varied sensory and motor aspects of the first and second brain, contributing much to our understanding of the gross and fine, afferent and efferent, control of image formation and expression.

The Autonomic Nervous System
THE SYMPATHETIC DIVISION

Every blood and lymphatic vessel, every sweat gland, endocrine gland, every tissue and organ in the body, including the brain itself, is linked, by afferent and efferent loops, with the core segments of the second and first brains: the control of the heartbeat, the heart's force of contraction, the breathing rate, the blood flow through every tissue, the muscles that modulate digestion and peristalsis and the muscles that dilate and constrict the pupil. No part of the body is forgotten in this pervasive monitoring, image building and modulatory control by the first and second brains. Rapid, finely-honed but large shifts in blood volume, both cyclic and urgent, occur in time intervals that are astonishing — each serving the varied survival prerogatives we outlined earlier.

Into this inner-circulating ocean, the glands associated with the second brain secrete a host of molecular forms; subtle images of causal, emotional states that circulate throughout the body, activating and deftly influencing the expressive capacity of each tissue and cell. In contrast to the immediate (microsecond) responses modulated by neural impulses, the molecular secretions are of a much more enduring influence; a fact that we subjectively experience in the relative persistence of many feeling states.

The central feature which we wish to emphasize is that the second brain creates both neural and molecular images of afferent and efferent types. For example, we can *feel* the rising within ourselves of irritability that may grow to become a state of anger. This is the formation of an afferent (input) image. The expression of anger, through vocal tension, aggressive bodily movements and the image moving across the face, literally reflects the efferent (output) image.

THE PARASYMPATHETIC DIVISION

The parasympathetic portion of the autonomic nervous system is almost wholly directed inwardly and is often spoken of as *opposing* the influence of the sympathetic nervous system (which is a particularly harmful and superficial perspective). This cranio-sacral amalgam of nerve cells is rooted in the first brain but blossoms into a potent *simultaneity* within the second brain. Through the head, neck and trunk extensions (but not the extremities) it demonstrates a primary body-sustaining influence by modulating the processes concerned with digestion, elimination, energy production and storage, tissue repair and sexual reproductive motor-erectile function. It is intimately entrained with the neural and molecular activities of the hypothalamus, contributing input and serving as the expressive output limb for images that, though difficult to describe, are readily recognized in our experience.

For example:

△ When, on one of those strikingly pleasant early spring days, one walks into the garden and finds oneself peering and gently prodding, looking for the first evidences of new life, one can become aware of a pervasive, strong but gentle, expectant atmosphere within oneself. As the first bud suddenly enters our visual field, a surge within this atmosphere – of expectation fulfilled, of hope come to actuality – is often experienced. This experience, a confirmation of renewal and of regeneration, melds into a continuity the subjective emotions of faith and hope, perhaps culminating in an ever-so-brief moment beyond either. The source, the resonating 'image' inside, which finds its confirmation in the appearance of the first flower bud, lies within the second brain – strongly fed by the nurturing, digesting, sustaining and procreative 'images' arising from the parasympathetic.

△ Each of us has experienced the feeling of vitality – of vibrant healthfulness and high-energy reserve, of readiness to take on a challenge. Clearly, this state has a strong sensory component; a pleasant sensation of known strength. However, it goes considerably beyond the sensory and this elusive but vibrant *e-motion* reflects a point of balance between the sympathetic (the energy-in-motion) and the parasympathetic (the energy-in-reserve). It is ready and willing.

All of the foregoing points of discussion play very important roles in the evolutionary appearance of the primordial relationship with other — the family.

THE FAMILY TRIAD
In his seminal and comprehensive volume entitled *The Triune Brain in Evolution*, Dr. Paul MacLean states:

> "In addition to endothermy, there were three cardinal behavioral developments that characterize the evolutionary transition from reptiles to mammals—namely, (1) nursing, in conjunction with maternal care; (2) audiovocal communication for maintaining maternal-offspring contact; and (3) play. Because of this unique family-related triad, one might say that the history of the evolution of the limbic system is the history of the evolution of mammals, while the history of the evolution of mammals is the history of the evolution of the family."[12]

Dr. MacLean's insight into the linkage between the evolution of the limbic system (part of the second brain) and the evolution of the family is of extraordinary importance, as we will consider when we take up the third brain. Suffice it to say that, in the future, fields as diverse as education, psychotherapeutics and international relations will be profoundly altered for the good by the application of his understanding.

The triad that MacLean refers to has a most interesting resonance with the survival triad of the second brain, as was noted earlier.

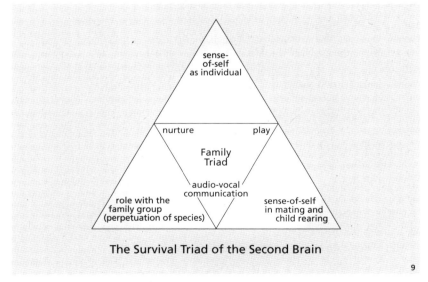

The Survival Triad of the Second Brain

The inner (family) triad comprises the functional behaviors that, taken together, underpin the appropriate manifestations of the three senses-of-self. The respective roles played out in life by all adult two-brained (mammalian) beings are infused, balanced and matured by the inner family triad.

---

12 Paul D. MacLean, *The Triune Brain in Evolution*, (New York: Plenum Press, 1990), p 247.

Summary

The achievements of the second brain are as equally astonishing as those of the first brain and occur in dimensions that carry two-brained creatures infinitely beyond one-brained life. Primary among these achievements is the coalescence of the inner and outer sensory images into the circumstance of awareness which we refer to as the sense-of-self-other. Mammalian life-forms explore the possibilities of self-other relationships in an almost infinite number of ways and, while a sense-of-I is not present in most two-brained life (high primates, dolphins and elephants being possible exceptions),[13] a world of valued, emotive relationships is clearly present.

We have intentionally provided only a brief glimpse of the structuring and imaging capacity of the second brain, hoping to interest and entice you into your own further explorations. The current literature in neurophysiology and the biological sciences is alive with fascinating confirmations of the imaging power and breadth of influence of the second brain.

Far more profound (because it relates to our everyday life), is Gurdjieff's representation—woven from talks, stories and sensation-picturings scattered throughout *Beelzebub's Tales to His Grandson*—but with particular appropriateness in the chapters on the Second, Third, and Fourth Descents, the planet Purgatory and Hypnotism.

The Third Brain—The Neocortex

Awareness, as a primal feature of brained life, has moved from and through an awareness of the external world (first brain) to include and harmonize with an awareness of the internal world (second brain). The evolving brain has been the primary instrument in an exploration by life which led first to a three-dimensional view of the outside world, which is wholly resonant (as event and process) with the forms and energies of that world. Similarly, a resonant three-dimensional view of the inside world emerges from the second brain's exploration, plus the *fused* moving-center manifestation of the possibilities and meanings of all self-other relationships.

> How can we speak of a third, equally infinite, exploration?
>
> What manner of afferent sensory receptors appears with the development of the third brain?
>
> What manifestations of its moving, efferent activity are possible and characteristic?
>
> Moreover, what are its images?
>
> Looking at early man, via archeological and anthropological evidence, we can ask, "What appears here that separates, by an infinite gulf, the cleverness, curiosity, communication skills and inventiveness of the high primates from the unique attribute(s) entering with the human third brain?"

---

[13] Findings by researches at the Yerkes National Primate Research Center, Emory University and The Wildlife Conservation Society of New York, published in *Science Daily*, October 2006.

What appeared, for us, came from recalling the primary emphasis Gurdjieff placed on "independent automatic" movement.[14] In *Perspectives*,[15] we explore at some length the application of this principle of *independent movement* to man's physical, emotional and intellectual life. Following the same line of thought, we asked ourselves, "What are the first wholed and completed events/processes that we can identify in the life of a human being that express a unique attribute, having the quality of an independent movement?"

Earlier, we identified three such independent movements, three forms of *mentation* — one each for man's physical, emotional and intellectual aspects.

Forms of Mentation

MacLean refers to three main *forms* of mentation.

Protomentation — (mentation of the physical body) rudimentary mental processes underlying special and general forms of behavior including four basic forms of prosematic communication. These rudimentary (but surprisingly complex and subtle) mental processes primarily characterize one-brained creatures and have their locus of organization in the reptilian-complex (striatal complex, including the caudate nucleus, putamen and the olfacto-striatum).

Emotional mentation — more complex processes that have their locus of organization in the limbic system (hippocampus-hypothalamus-amygdala and cingulate gyrus). This fusion of internal and external sensory-motor systems underpins endothermy, intrauterine development and the appearance of nurturing, audio-vocal communication and play as distinguishing markers of self-other, two-brained life.

Rational mentation — ratiocination or the deduction of conclusions from premises. This is the domain of the third brain (neocortex). MacLean emphasizes the process of "deduction of conclusions from premises." This principle is what underpins the human capacity to come to speech and language, although we are discovering that it is a multi-stepped and enormously complex process which involves the compounding and coalescing of many smaller ratiocinations and abstractions.

The *new perspective* and the resulting capacities that flow from that perspective (what we referred to earlier as the third brain's unique attribute) and Dr. MacLean's "rational mentation" are simply two expressions of the same uniqueness. We prefer to speak of it from the triadic viewing noted in (illustration 10) because it allows a neurophysiological process of the fusion of three levels of *imaging* to account for the remarkable deductive capacity of the third brain. The establishment of the three earliest *independent motions*, 1) bipedal gait, 2) self-assertion and 3) speech and language, requires this deductive capacity just as surely as, generations later, man began to fashion tools and eventually to build bridges and intercontinental ballistic missiles; to write poetry and to make computers.

14 Gurdjieff, *Beelzebub's Tales*, p 762.
15 Buzzell, *Perspectives*, chapter 11, "The Emergence of Individual Reason," pp 171-89.

Physical

As parents we all delight (at least temporarily) in our child's first independent steps. Bipedal locomotion is the first, wholed event/process that shows itself as a defining marker of humanness. We can ask "What is it, in neurophysiological terms, that makes this possible?"

There is considerable evidence that, lacking bipedal modeling by other humans, a young child will not walk; in the few instances reported (of young children being terribly isolated for the first two years of life), they never learned to walk with the natural gait characteristic of an adult. Modeling of bipedal gait seems, then, a near absolute prerequisite. This requires a highly sophisticated sensory imaging system that combines the outer and inner sensory-motor capacities of the first and second brain.

However, the higher primates have such a system and, in their natural growth sequence, do not adopt a preferred independent bipedal locomotion as do humans.

There are also certain physical alterations, i.e., the shape of the lumbar spine, pelvis, hip, knee and ankle/foot that are distinguishing features of modern humans (as well as evolved changes in the rest of the spine and shoulder girdle). Although early man did not have these appendicular alterations to the well-differentiated degree of modern man, he was, nonetheless, truly bipedal.

The third and defining neurophysiological attribute, that both drives and enables the infant to come to "independent automatic" movement, is the new perspective and the resulting capacities flowing from that perspective. From reptilian life through early mammalian forms, it has been demonstrated that ablation or removal of the cerebral hemispheres (however thin a layer this may be in reptiles like the lizard) renders the creature unable to initiate or carry on spontaneous, directed behavior. As MacLean notes,

> "The remaining brainstem and spinal cord constitute a neural chassis that provides most of the neural machinery required for self-preservation and the preservation of the species. By itself, the neural chassis might be likened to a vehicle without a driver. Significantly, in the more advanced vertebrates the evolutionary process has provided the neural chassis not with a single guiding operator, but rather a combination of three; each markedly different in its evolutionary age and development and each radically different in structure, chemistry and organization."[16]

Beyond the initiation of spontaneous directed behavior, the *human* third brain has the capacity to view the function of the other two brains from an *independent* perspective. This point is imaged in the illustration on the following page (figure 10).

---

16 MacLean, *The Triune Brain in Evolution*, P 23.

The Triune Brain

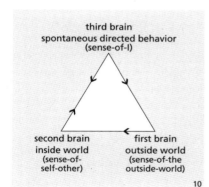

The viewing from this perspective is not meant to imply a fully conscious, self-initiating capacity. Rather, this is a mechanical, *half-awake* state, which is subjectively experienced as a sense-of-I, a singularity. It is a result of a fusion of the neurophysiological, triadic imagings of the three brains.

In the human infant, this three-dimensional perspective brings with it, by neurophysiological law, the capacity to image (to unconsciously understand) the physical laws of moving through space on two limbs. By persistent trial and error, in imitation of surrounding bipedal elders, the required thrustings – holdings – balancings are gradually organized, by the capacity of the third brain, into a dense associative pattern. As parents, the result is our enthusiastic celebration of the attainment of independent bipedal locomotion by our children. Indeed, it is an appropriate celebration because it marks, as mentioned earlier, the first, wholed event/process of our human uniqueness.

By no means does the foregoing imply that a non-walking child, as a result of genetic, traumatic or infectious insults, is other than wholly human. It does illustrate, however, the first, externally manifested capacity that flows outward from within the child as a wholly independent and completed event/process.

Emotional

Some parents do not celebrate the first wholed event/process, in the *second-brain* life of the child, with a fervor equal to that celebrated with the appearance of bipedal locomotion,

Here, the emotional *self-assertion* of the young child appears as a completed process and is often referred to as the "terrible twos." This development reflects the emerging independent motion in the emotional world of humans.

The third brain, from its new perspective, comes to see and unconsciously understand that its second-brain life of self-other can be independently experienced and moved from. Many other mammals, especially the high primates, show, in their childhood play, a tentative movement toward this emotionally-based independent motion. Nevertheless, none comes to possess it as a permanent attribute.

At an essentially causal level, we can say that a child begins to see that it can manipulate the laws of self-other relationships in its own favor (those laws that, neurophysiologically, find their varied and sophisticated expressions via the limbic system of mammals).

Intellectual

The third, externally demonstrated *independent motion* (that wholed event/process establishing the third dimension of the chasm separating human from other mammalian life), is the attainment of speech. Hundreds of thousands of neurophysiological mentation events precede this external manifestation.

The sounds of words, vocal play, organization of patterns of sound, the process of symbolizing and the directed, self-other correspondences — each and all of these involve immensely dense associative 'workings-out' in various parts of the cortical and the sub-cortical centers. PET scanning, functional MRI imaging and other electro-physiological testing methods are just beginning to demonstrate the form and sequence of this immensely complex process. When firmly and finally established as a wholed capacity, it becomes the external marker most often referred to as distinguishing human from all other life.

TOOL-MAKING

What does it mean to make a tool? It means to have the capacity, by seeing analogies, to understand physical relationships and through that, to see a form of law.

The high primates have the capacity to see (to image) in analogy, to know that "this is like that." However, they cannot see the relationship and come, through that abstracting process, to image physical law.

To see relationship (or to see 'this *and* that' and what connects them functionally) and then be able to *whole* the lawful factors that bind separated events and/or motions (functions) together — this is the gift of the third brain.

That it would show itself first through the body in bipedal gait is a beautiful, compacted image of man's primordial capacity to truly change the world. No matter that it will take four million years (or less, depending on one's interpretation of early hominid differentiation) to reach the present era and the overwhelming evidence that man not only can, but has, changed the whole of the planet.

IMAGES-OF-LAW

We have tried to look at and sift through the historical evidence of man's activities, then to measure the plethora of changes from tools to clothes to weapons and from caves to mud huts to high rises; from the earliest carvings to the Taj Mahal; from the earliest vocalizations to symphonic music; from hunter-gatherer to agriculture and the domestication of animals. Always, this capacity to see and form *images-of-law* through the capacity of directing our attention appears as the defining attribute ~ the 'enzyme' that catalyzes man's physical, emotional and intellectual activities as a *newness*, which is the wide chasm separating three-brained beings from all other life.

The wheel, bridge, plow and pendulum are results of the imaging-of-law into the physical world. The same capacity, applied to sounds, (e.g., grunts, mews, squeals, whinnies, clucks and roars), underpins the appearance of sound images or sounds-that-stand-for objects and motions. From this, elemental language appears. Later, when the relationship (the law) between sound images and hand-molded symbols (another form of image-of-law) is seen, written language, in forms that reflect the unique experiences of isolated groups of people, begins to appear. Later yet, as the abstracting process in symbolic form continues to develop and coalesce, we see the appearance of counting, mathematics and, finally, abstract physical law (of motion, friction, gases, gravity, etc.).

From each seeing-of-law (however small), a vast horizon of possibilities opens to man and he plunges into each new landscape – exploring, testing and inventing; moving into nooks and crannies in a manner analogous to the physical and emotional (social) explorations of one- and two-brained beings.

A major difference is that man, from his third brain, moves into the physical, emotional and intellectual worlds simultaneously and, with this, brings a new order of infinite possibilities. The infinity of the physical (macromolecular) world and the infinity of the emotional (atmospheric-molecular) world, has been opened to the potential reconciliation of the true intellectual world.[17]

With this power to image law comes the enablement of the moving-center's expression of this *seeing* — and man's two-brained curiosity and inventiveness is raised to a level of cleverness, manipulation and creativity that has been unstoppable in its continuing manifestation.

THE HAZARD

With the second brain, the sense-of-self-other appeared as a subjective image and was reconciled by the world-of-other, (e.g., of herd, flock, den, pride or colony) in hierarchically established roles. Two-brained creatures evolve under causal law (hard-wired) and become ~ in all respects ~ a harmonious part of the greater whole of life on Earth.

The capacity to image lawful, physical relationships appears (however narrow its initial focus) on the leading edge of the continent of the third brain. When man moves rapidly toward the interior of this new continent, however, an immensely potent and hazardous image begins to appear.

Via the energy that flows from the evolving capacity to image relationship to physical law, the sense-of-self-other of the second brain is *added to* by the sense-of-I of the third brain. In this, a great hazard emerges – for the sense-of-I is not the *real* I that Gurdjieff so impeccably gives us a progressive vision of in *Beelzebub's Tales to His Grandson*. It is, rather, a self-created image of 'I' that is the consequence of the third brain's capacity to relate three physical (or mechanical) aspects of an event or process into a lawful *one*. The 'sense-of-the-world-outside' (first brain) and the 'sense-of-the-world-inside' (the sense-of-self-other of the second brain) are coalesced into a 3. The new sense of the 3 is not of a separated 3 (as having both clearly separated and yet interdependent parts), but of a united 3; a kind of *1* — the *sense-of*-I.

---

17 This is a concept parallel to that of the mathematician George Cantor's aleph 0,1, and 2.

We are all familiar with the observation of a small 'I' of the moment. Important emphasis is placed by Work on *seeing* the three aspects of each of these little 'I's; the physical sensations and bodily movements, the feeling and its physical manifestation through gesture, facial expression, tone of voice and the 'a-thinking' (mechanical associations). Initially, we are instructed and assisted in observing these aspects separately. However, as our attention and capacity increase, we are brought to a simultaneous viewing of two and, eventually, all three aspects.

One of the most essential observations, which arises and is confirmed by this simultaneous viewing, is that our three parts are most often not harmonized or truly reconciled into a resonant *one* but are at odds with each other. The sense-of-self-other (emotional) is not resonant with sensations or thoughts, or the sense-of-I stands bewildered by the opposing images presented by the first and second brains. Yet, we say "I" in the presence of this disharmonious *three*, because our third brain is obliged, by appropriate and harmonious law, to image the three aspects as *one*.

The hazard we noted earlier lies precisely in this paradox. The emerging third brain, in spite of its remarkable power to image *physical* relationships to law with respect to the outside or material world, *does not have a high enough energy at its initial disposal* to image appropriate and resonant *emotional* (the second brain) relationships to law. This is such an important point that we will go into it in further detail.

The second brain explores the world of self-other relationships and, in mammalian life-forms, we find great diversity in the causal, determined solutions to self-group relationships. In mammalian life, successful solutions are measured by their persistence and balance with respect to the total environmental circumstances in which they arise. There are, thus, many appropriate solutions – each lawfully determined – over long time periods.

However, the imaging capacity of the third brain introduces a new and causally unforeseeable consequence, which is that the understanding of physical law and the immense powers that, over time, accrue to the individual being, will be an increasingly potent carrier of force in the imaging of the sense-of-I.

The sense-of-I, gaining increasing power in the physical world, runs the formidable risk of using this power to determine new and non-resonant forms of self-other (second brain) relationships. These new forms would not be founded upon causal, survival-of-the-group-through-hierarchically-patterned roles, but could introduce personal and social hierarchies based upon the increasing knowledge of physical laws and the individual willingness to use this knowledge to empower the individual sense-of-I.

Thus, the possibility of:

~ **egoism** — the sense-of-I that increasingly narrows the breadth of all first- and second-brain functions to a focal point of *imagined* self-significance and,

~ master/slave — an unforeseen, man-made and, in terms of cosmic law, *unlawful* hierarchy; one that places all three-brained beings in positions of inferiority or superiority based upon an *un-wholed* image of personal and social relationships.

The third brain of man is, therefore, the germinal influence in the vention of the Baroque organ and of the medieval torture rack, of the Hubble Telescope and of stealth bombers. The critical difference lies in how the *hazard* – implicit in the third brain's capacity to image physical law – is resolved.

If its potency becomes imploded and dedicated to a first brain self-preservation-of-the-physical-body, then the destructive power of the third brain is immense in the material world. If the same imploded potency becomes dedicated to a "topsy-turvy," egoistic view of self-other relationships (second brain), then a master/slave circumstance results with all the elements of a caste system.

The third brain's capacity is real and externally creative. It can and does lead to a near infinitude of external (physical) expressions. What separates these external expressions into two large but opposite manifestations depends on whether the implicit hazard is reconciled by an aggressively selfish sense-of-I (with or without a master/slave condition) or by a sense-of-I that has been encouraged and enabled by familial, cultural and spiritual values which, simultaneously, allows for the individual uniqueness of the third brain, while modeling more wholesome and balanced self-other relationships.

We can point to a multitude of harmonious expressions of the unique qualities of man's third brain: from early tool making to the construction of a Stradivarius; from whistles and flutes to the multi-keyboarded organs of Bach's time; from folk songs and epic poetry to the symphony; from the cave paintings of Lascaux to French Impressionism; from the earliest tabulations of grain stocks to Euclid, Newton, Einstein and Schrödinger. In this cornucopia of more balanced manifestations of man's third brain, there are endless verifications of the potency to-image-law. The incredible variety of manifestations illustrates the outcomes of the third brain's penetration into and through the first and second brains, as well as its own singular capacity *to see, to know* and *to form abstractions* of that knowing.

In contrast, we can point to all conquerors, from Alexander to Hitler and Stalin, and from Attila the Hun and the Spanish Conquistadors to the warlords who presently infect Somalia and Darfur. Each (and a multitude of others that could be named) has come to their 'privileged' place by using the formidable potency of the third brain to image unlawful relationships between the first, second and third brains of others, as well as of their own. A destructive power, with enormous and long-term consequences, is released when the *false* sense-of-I implodes and dedicates its third-brain capacity to hierarchizing all other beings into an imaginary world of dependent relationships which ultimately support the presumed significance of this imploded sense-of-I.

On a smaller scale, we ordinary people also demonstrate this third-brain capacity to put our sense-of-I on an imaginary pedestal. For example:

- ~ when we are authoritatively and inarguably 'right'!
- ~ when we demand that our children obey because,
"I am your father!"
- ~ when we cleverly insinuate (but, oh so gently!) that,
"those people just don't have what it takes!"
- ~ when we demand to have our pleasure, knowing there
will be others for whom it will bring pain;
- ~ when our passion for justice demands that certain people
(or animals or birds) simply have to be sacrificed because
they are too old, too cruel or too non-productive–because
the 'greater good' requires it.

What separates the petty egoist of everyday life from a terrifying monster like Hitler or Stalin seems, sadly, to be a quantitative rather than a qualitative factor. We have only to look at the dimensions of the physical, emotional and sexual abuse of children in this country to see clearly how far the plunge into egoistic malevolence can be within personal and family relationships.

Seeing this, we need only magnify the opportunity for such malevolent activity to see how it can grow to encompass communities and nations.

We mentioned earlier how the simultaneous process of *experimentation* and *modeling relationships* of the emerging third brain is essential for its harmonious development. This would apply whether viewed in terms of a young child or a young culture. The aim of this experimenting/modeling is to enable a youthful third brain to avoid the hazards of egoism and master/slave, and to grow toward more harmoniously creative, personal and social expressions of its capacities.

Historically, the sources of these enabling influences are referred to as "the Great Traditions"—those spiritual and philosophical impulses that have periodically entered the life of humanity and brought with them images of appropriate and harmonious relationships which span the personal, familial, social and spiritual aspects of human life.

Sadly—these influences, because they are, at their point of origin, essentially benign, compassionate and respectful, have each been rapidly invaded and usurped by those whose motivations derive from egoism and master/slave perspectives.

The result has always led to a rapid (in cultural time) dilution and distortion of the enabling influences of the Great Traditions, producing, in our modern instantaneously-linked one-world, a sorrowful arena of fixed attitudes, absolutist beliefs and social caste systems, more in keeping with the rigid paranoia and reflexive aggression of a one-brained lizard than with the stated and initially modeled aims of the Great Traditions.

THE SCIENTIFIC METHOD

With the Renaissance there appeared, in germinal form, that method of enquiry that has become known as "the scientific method." Of all the imagings-of-physical-law[18] that have flowed from the inborn capacity of the third brain, this has become, far and away, the most powerful, both in insights into the material world and in the technological means to alter that world.

With the unstoppable penetration of the scientific method and its technological effluent into every aspect of the physical world has come an equally accelerating crescendo of the hazard. As we look around our world today, we find countless examples of man's third-brain egoism and master/slave propensities making powerful and malevolent use of the effluent of the scientific method. From rifles to intercontinental ballistic missiles and, from mustard gas to modern bacteriological weapons, we see graphic and horrifying images of the perversion by egoism of some of man's highest capacities.

The Positive Aspect

However, the scientific method, in its purest sense of "enquiry into the nature and laws of the physical world,"[19] can be, and has been, used as a potent, creative and healing model by the third brain of man. Man's images-of-law (formulae and principles) have been the source of each of his truly creative and compassionate manifestations. We can trace a multitude of these images-given-form in the physical, emotional, intellectual and spiritual life of man. One of the sources lies with the introduction of perspective in painting which brought a three-dimensional viewing of our world that broke through the rigid art of the Middle Ages. In parallel with this new fundamental understanding of light, depth and shadow, came a new perspective on *time*[20] and the relationship of multiple objects to each other, in motion and at rest, as well as the varied, three-dimensional appearances of objects when a viewer moves in relation to the object. These new images, leading to harmonious and proportionate representation in space and time, became the germinal notions of the scientific method. From the Renaissance through the 20th century, man has accumulated and woven together thousands of images-of-law, slowly accreting and integrating a vast warehouse of observations and experiments into simpler, more encompassing and elegant images.

Newton's *Principia*, Einstein's special and general theories of relativity and Schrödinger's quantum mechanical principles are examples of the simultaneous coalescence of varied prior images and the appearance of new and more inclusive ones. These images-of-law take on form in the cornucopia of inventions and creative manifestations of the past six hundred years. Taller buildings and longer bridges, made possible by verifiable (formulaic) images-

---

18 e.g., $m=f/a$ where m=mass, f=force, a=acceleration or $F=Gmm^1/d^2$ where F=force, G=the gravitational constant, mm^1=the product of the masses of bodies and d=distance
19 *Funk and Wagnalls Standard College Dictionary*
20 The artistic exploration of the third dimension (perspective) led to a deeper appreciation of motion and distance. The study of velocity (distance covered in a specified *time*) introduced an increasing appreciation of the role of time in human perspectives on change.

of-law, not only alter the social life of man in radical ways but also provide opportunities for artisans and crafts people to explore and manifest their creative images. The appearance of the steam engine and, later, the internal combustion engine, completely revolutionized the motions of humanity, including the resultant artistic and social perspectives.

Analyzing the changes in musical forms that occur from the time of Palestrina and Monteverdi through the densely contrapuntal, chromatic style of the Baroque and from the Classical school of Vienna to Mozart, Beethoven and the Romantic and Neoclassical schools, it is quite astonishing to note the parallels in 'image' that move through science, technology, social forms, fashion and the arts. It is as if the successive images-of-law are reflected through infinitely varied and individualized three-brained beings – moving, exploring, compounding the images of the past and occasionally striking out in new directions. These new viewings soon led to analogies in other fields apparently quite distant from the initial viewings. For example, the mechanistic and deterministic views of early 19th century science find their way rapidly into the poetry, music, architecture, fashion and sociological/psychological perspectives of the latter 19th and early 20th century. Likewise, the music, poetry, social forms and psychological systems of our present day reflect the imaging-in-law brought by relativity and quantum mechanical theory.

Given the inveterate exploratory and creative capacity of the *triune brain* and the hazards of egoism lying within man's third brain, we are brought to the focal question of this chapter.

How can we approach a true reconciliation, a digestion – exploration – new creation, that has the realistic hope of healing our fragmenting, egoistic, all too single-brained world of "peculiar"[21] three-brained beings?

An adequate approach to this primordial question must, simultaneously, harmonize and integrate the following images-of-law:

- △ that everything, every state of matter or energy, every idea, feeling and motion in our entire Cosmos is interconnected (webbed and woofed) into one great moving *whole*;
- △ that this interconnectedness is not an abstract, indifferent, mechanical process but is, rather, an endless, multi-layered feeding – sustaining – nurturing;
- △ that since everything is essential and has its roles to fulfill within the whole, everything is to be valued in balanced proportion;
- △ that the balanced proportion can only be approached if man's third brain is constantly alerted to and reminded of the real hazards of egoism and master/slave and enabled to explore and create new and more harmonious personal (first brain) and social (second brain) images-in-law.

---

21 Gurdjieff, *Beelzebub's Tales,* there are many references to "peculiar" throughout the text.

How can this be accomplished?

Is the foregoing an unrealistic, idealistic daydream?

If so, then we can only encourage you to consider, with care and sobriety, the world inside and outside of us. Consider the uncountable civil wars and the unremitting, increasing weight of suffering of the mothers and children of our world. Consider our greed, paranoia and one-brained, 'take care of myself' attitudes. Consider what we have done to this beautiful, fragile planet. Is this what we wish for our children and for all children to come?

It is well past time for us to wonder, ponder and act on the question asked by the sage, Mullah Nassr Eddin in Gurdjieff's *First Series*, "People! People! Why are you people?" [22]

In Sum...

Life can be viewed as a persisting, transformative and self-regenerative *whole* that maintains its wholeness by holding, in lawful relationship, a variable but harmonious mix of material–energies of the photonic, atomic, electronic and molecular-macromolecular worlds. The appearance and the development of sensory-motor-associative systems (brains) exemplifies life's expanding capacity to be active from within its individuated life-forms, in contrast to the essentially passive capacities we see reflected in microcosmoses, multi-celled and surplanetary life-forms (all non-brained). Independent motions — whether first-brained/physical, second-brained/emotional or third-brained/intellectual — appear with each *brain*, coupled to sensory systems appropriate to the three motions and are reconciled by a central imaging–associating–patterning and directing whole.

As each brain appears it brings not only wholly new afferent–integrative–efferent capacities but also interpenetrates the previously arisen brain, enriching and expanding its capacities to remarkable degrees. With each infinitely large step, a new *whole* is the consequence ~ each fulfilling an essential arena of roles in the complexities of all life-forms.

These are roles that fundamentally concern the entry, exploration and establishment of increasing degrees of *awareness* of the three worlds which are outside, inside and beyond life itself. With the entry of the *awarenesses* deriving from the capacities of the third brain, comes also the potential discovery of true sincerity, conscience and understanding ~ leading to wisdom. These steps bring us to the threshold of what Gurdjieff refers to as Kesdjan Body, Higher-being Body and Objective Reason ~ considerations that are the central focus and pinnacle of possibility in Work.

---

22 Gurdjieff, *Beelzebub's Tales*, p 1023.

CHAPTER 2 PAGE 26 ENDNOTES

I Gurdjieff, *Beelzebub's Tales*, p 143.

II Ibid., p 144.

III MacLean, *The Triune Brain in Evolution*, p 14.

"The physical world is entirely abstract and without 'actuality' apart from its linkage to consciousness."[I]

"In introspection, it is clearly impossible to distinguish sharply between the phenomena themselves and their conscious perception."[II]

"The ultimate creative principle is consciousness. There are different levels of consciousness. What we call innermost subtle consciousness is always there.... All of our other [kinds of] consciousness – sense consciousness and so on – arise in dependence on this mind of clear light."[III]

CHAPTER 3
CONSCIOUSNESS AS THE COALESCENCE OF IMAGES

While reading the current and rapidly expanding literature about human consciousness, one could conclude that, just as Athena sprang fully armed from the cloven skull of Zeus, this singular attribute appeared, *de novo*, with the arrival of man. The assumption that human consciousness is unique and has no clearly defined precursor states or that it owes little to the five hundred million years of brained life that preceded its evolution, reflects a prejudicial view of reptilian and mammalian awarenesses (and their associated processes of mentation) which seems unduly anthropocentric and quite at odds with the evolutionary evidence.

In contrast, human consciousness can be viewed as the culmination of an exceedingly long and many-layered *braining* process that occurred in direct continuity with the evolution of invertebrate, vertebrate and mammalian life. Viewed from this perspective, the fundamental question becomes, "What was the elemental attribute of brained activity from which, over five hundred million years, it is possible to trace the progressive development and differentiation of what has become, as a natural evolutionary unfolding, human consciousness?"

We posit that this elemental attribute was the evolved capacity of the first (or core) brain to construct moving images (resonant representations or likenesses) of a portion of the energies and forms that lie at and beyond the external surface of the creature.

A Great *Turning*

When brained life appeared on the Earth some 500 million years ago, a Great Turning took place in the evolution of the material Universe as well as in organic life. From the Initial Moment and throughout the early expansion phase, each and every process of nucleosyntheses, early galactic formation and the condensation of our Sun (a period encompassing 10-12 billion years) took place in accordance with physical law. No motions of protons stars or galaxies took place *independently* Even the motions and interactions that took place in the primeval oceans were determined motions and interactions. The temperature ranges, ionic composition and concentration in the oceans, the radiation levels in the atmosphere, as well as the magma flow beneath tectonic plates—all of these physical aspects interacted in accordance with fundamental physical law. Even the initial appearance of life, in the form of the archaebacteria, can be understood in a context of unfolding, complex, lawful actions that mediated subtle interactions between accidentally but lawfully produced amino acids and RNA fragments.

Nowhere and at no time in this multi-billion year process was there a confluence-of-law that would produce a *witness* to all that was happening. The Universe, in each of its parts and in its entirety, could be described as being deaf and blind, unable to touch, taste or smell *itself*. With no created agencies that could form resonant representations or images, nothing at all could be *sensed*.

For even the simplest of images to appear, a multitude of uni-celled and then multicellular life-forms had to evolve, prepare and refine the substrate biological mechanisms necessary for a brained existence. This preparatory time encompassed three to three and a half billion years.

When a brained being finally evolved, it did so within an uninterrupted flow of physical law. With no intervention or changing of physical law required to explain the emergence of a brain, it is appropriate to say that, at the Initial Moment, a context determined by primal laws permitted the possibility that a life-form could appear within the Creation that had the elemental capacity to image aspects of the Creation of which it was a product.

The use of the word "witness" and the allusion to sensory and motor systems are most often understood as applying to human witnesses and human sensory-motor systems. What may be left aside, as relatively insignificant, is the fact that one- and two-brained creatures (invertebrate, vertebrate and mammalian) have existed on the Earth for 500 million years—compared to man's 2.5 to 4 million years. Said differently, for 99 per cent of the time that brained beings have been present, they have been one- and two-brained only. Uncountable images of earth's surfaces and oceans were created by that quintessential process of building resonant representations of the forms and energies present on and within the earth.

Having formed imaging instruments that construct representations of the world beyond the boundary membrane of the body, brain evolution later *turned* within and developed imaging instruments that, over time, became capable of constructing resonant representations of the inner world of the body itself. These instruments and their associative neural nets and motor efferents are now referred to as the second or limbic brain.

The unique imaging capacities of the first and second brain became never-ending sources of feedback. The feedback itself became a powerful determining factor in the evolution of all brained beings, including man. One aspect of the Great Turning was the constancy of these feedback loops. What creatures can image, and how well they do so in comparison to others, became a prime survival capacity. This applies to each sense (outer and inner) and to their various combinations. For many species, the higher refinement of these imaging instruments and their complementary associative and motor aspects appear to be the single, most powerful survival advantage they have.

INDEPENDENT AUTOMATIC MOTION

Simultaneous with the evolution of the afferent-associative-imaging capacities,[1] and linked to it by complex feedback loops, is the evolution of efferent-motor capacities. No survival advantage would accrue to a creature unless both ends of this neural pendulum underwent simultaneous and continuing self-feedback development. By self-feedback is meant the real-time, repetitious sensory-associative-motor processes that occur within a given creature over time. These associative processes (the gradual organization of which underpin the appearance of what MacLean refers to as the instinctive master routines and subroutines),[2] with progressive refinements and linkages that can be traced through evolutionary time, contain and express the overall form and lawful sequence which unfolds all three brains.

One result of this braining process is the first appearance, in the entire creation to that time, of "independent automatic moving ... on the surface of the given planets."[3] That a multicellular life-form could come to a relative degree of self-determined movement through the agency of a self-contained sensory-imaging-associative-motor instrument (a brain) is another way of characterizing the Great Turning.

This principle has been recognized for at least several thousand years. Thales (600 BC) maintained that the ability to initiate movement is a key attribute of life. "Like Thales, Aristotle considered that the existential quality of living creatures was that they possessed their own internal will and this allowed creatures to initiate independent movement."[4]

---

1 Clearly, the evolution of the brain is intimately related to evolutionary processes taking place in other parts of the body. For example, the evolution of the human neocortex, of the hand, larynx, pelvis, and shoulder joint occur within an incredibly dense matrix of feedback loops, each of which carries opportunities, challenges and limitations. While our focus is on brain evolution, it is not our intention to diminish the importance of multiple evolutionary strands.
2 MacLean, *The Triune Brain in Evolution*, see the glossary and recommended reading.
3 Gurdjieff, *Beelzebub's Tales*, p 762.
4 MacFadden, Johnjoe. *Quantum Evolution* (London: W.W. Norton, 2000), p 8.

Gurdjieff emphasizes the primal importance of this Great Turning when, in the chapter "The Holy Planet 'Purgatory'," he notes:

> "The point is that when the 'common-cosmic-harmonious-equilibrium' had become regularized and established in all those cosmoses of different scales, then in each of these Tetartocosmoses, i.e., in each separate 'relatively-independent-formation-of-the-aggregation-of-microcosmoses' which had its arising on the surface of the planets—the surrounding conditions on the surface of which accidentally began to correspond to certain data present in these cosmoses, owing to which they could exist for a certain period of time without what is called 'Seccruano,' i.e., without constant 'individual tension'—the possibility appeared of independent automatic moving from one place to another on the surface of the given planets.
>
> "And thereupon, when our COMMON FATHER ENDLESSNESS ascertained this automatic moving of theirs, there then arose for the first time in HIM the Divine Idea of making use of it as a help for HIMSELF in the administration of the enlarging World.
>
> "From that time on HE began to actualize everything further for these cosmoses ... ."[5]

This relative independence derives from the self-containment (within the physical body of the creature) of a three-dimensional, imaging-motor capability. No law of physics is broken in this process; what appear are separate, individuated, multi-sensed processing-reacting units (one-brained beings). No two creatures with brains wake up at the same moment, feed in exactly the same way, move, fight or mate at the same time or in the same environmental circumstances—even when the focal stimulus appears to be the same. The result is that each creature comes, in the flow of its unique history, to different *wholed* images, different experiences and different learnings. By "wholed" is meant the fusion of the different sensory images into one experiential event.

One-brained creatures do not have a great deal of behavioral flexibility. They are essentially hard-wired with relatively rigid routines, which Paul MacLean has outlined in detail. However, they are not predictable creatures. For example, the degree to which the behavior of two lizards differs in a given circumstance is partially due to the unique histories of each. The imaged patterns of external forms, energies and motions, become, in the flow of time, a unique experience. This experience (their learning) can be remembered to a limited degree. The memory of one-brained creatures is qualitatively different from the memory of two- and three-brained creatures, largely because there is no neural basis for a *sense of personal identity* in the R-complex (core of the first brain). Personal identity, or the sense-of-self-other, can only emerge when interceptors or inner senses begin to develop with the (second) limbic brain and continue their subtle image construction with the appearance of the third brain (neocortex). As MacLean comments,

---

5 Gurdjieff, *Beelzebub's Tales*, p 762.

> "... the condition that psychologically most clearly distinguishes us as individuals is our twofold source of information from the internal private world and the external public world."[6]

Lacking sources of information from the internal world, the memory processes of one-brained creatures are neither reinforced by, nor crystallized around, a separated experiencing whole (the sense-of-self). The result is a near total lack of flow or continuity between events – there being no *one* to carry that experiential flow.

One-brained creatures do learn, but their learning is firmly anchored to the space they inhabit and the objects and creatures around them. Empowered by the survival triad of 1) staying alive in the moment, 2) finding food, 3) finding a mate and patterned by hard-wired master routines and sub-routines, a lizard quickly learns all features and boundaries of its territory. If it did not, it could not find its way home or retreat to places of escape when threatened. Neither could it make known its display post, nor recognize the difference between a stranger and a member of the group. Most essentially, as MacLean notes, "experiential learning and memory become an indissociable addition to an animal's natural capacity for the practice of deceptive behavior."[7] It is in the deceptive behavior of one-brained beings where we see most clearly the intimation of a future that is not yet wholly determined in the one-brained world. The consequence of the deception cannot be known in the moment. A possibility is present but unrealized and thus, the result will be determined, in part, by the cleverness of the deception. Perhaps, this act is a foretaste of play that later becomes a primordial aspect of the life of mammals.

The world of one-brained creatures is, thus, a unique, experiential world but one which provides no evidence of a separated and subjective awareness. Its independence of motion, while conditional, is real and derives from its singular, personal history. Its flowing history, in turn, derives from the unique sensory-imaging-associative-motor capacity of its brain.

BECOMING CONSCIOUS OF A THREE-DIMENSIONAL WORLD

The development of multi-sense imaging abilities leads, in independently moving one-brained beings, to a remarkable synthesis of the energies and forms of the external world (illustrations 1 and 2 on pages 69-70).

△ **Vision** — The visible portion of the electromagnetic spectrum, largely in the frequency range of 4000 to 7000 Angströms, is resonantly represented in image by the visual system. Proportionality is the key to this and all other imaging processes; the transformative membrane of the retina reconstructs, through neural impulses, a relatively proportionate representation of varying concentrations of certain frequencies of light entering the eye. From these encoded patterns of neural impulses, the brain (via its visual associative apparatus) recreates a three-dimensional image of the pattern of reflected light.

---

6   MacLean, *The Triune Brain in Evolution*, from the Introduction.
7   Ibid., p 149.

Photons activate electrons into higher energy orbits and the transfer of these electrons is the energy source that leads, after multiple steps, to a propagated wave of ionic motions (the nerve impulse). The *re*-patterning (the giving of form) of these impulses by the visual center is the final step in the visual imaging process. The exact *how* of this step is one of the questions currently under intense study and research. Later in this chapter, we will outline a process that appears to be consistent with our fundamental thesis.

In the process of the development of the sense of vision, the separated but linked *worlds* of photons, electrons, ions (atoms), electromagnetic fields and micromolecules have been reconciled or blended by life into a remarkable mechanism.

△ **Hearing** — Sound waves are also transformed, by a complex sensory membrane, into patterned neural impulses. Again, the steps involve multiple levels of energies and forms. A living membrane (macromolecular-cellular ear drum) is set into a resonant vibration with the waveforms transmitted through the external medium. A bony (macromolecular) linkage transfers these vibrations to a membrane directly in continuity with a fluid (micro-molecular/macromolecular) medium. The waveforms in the fluid medium of the cochlea set tiny hairs in motion, which is proportionate to the wavelength and intensity of the initial sound waves. The hair-like projections are cellular extensions and, at their bases, the movement of the hair is transformed proportionately, via the piezoelectric principle (glossary), into the transfer of electrons. From here on, the sequential steps parallel those seen in visual processing – by utilizing ionic, micromolecular and electromagnetic field forces to create a resonant representation (an image) of the initiating pattern of the sound waves.

△ **Smell** — The sense of smell engages the world of stereotactic (three-dimensional) molecular forms. The transformative membrane is based on multi-patterns of molecular binding sites.[8] The odor molecules in the air, once dissolved in the thin mucoid layer overlying the olfactory receptor cells and their cilia, undergo selective binding at receptor sites. The binding itself appears related to the stereotactic form of the odor molecule and to electronic bonding energies. Once bonding occurs, the proportionality in the stimulation of neural impulses is maintained by intracellular, micromolecular and ionic (cAMP and Ca^{++} and Cl^-) energy transfers that result in the depolarization wave of the neural impulse itself. Within the olfactory bulb and cortex, a resonant representation (an image) in smells is created. This image, while vastly different from a visual image, nevertheless has a three-dimensional quality to it. Humans, with only seven million olfactory cells, cannot appreciate the dimensional quality to the degree to which it is appreciated in wolves, who have 260 million olfactory cells. For the wolf, the space it inhabits and moves through is permeated by nuances of odor, qualifying the species, age, sex and the direction of movement and proximity of many of the life-forms within surprisingly long distances. An image of the space it inhabits truly emerges for the wolf from its sense of smell.

---

8   These are the seven gene families.

△ **Taste**—Analogously, the sense of taste also constructs an image but this image is rooted in the macromolecular world and initially registered via the ionic or molecular. The sensory receptor cells, located in the tongue and other parts of the mouth, are responsive to four distinct qualities (sweet, salt, sour and bitter), but the energy-form aspects are our primary focus. Here protons (H+), potassium, sodium and calcium ions, micromolecular energy forms of ATP>AMP and specific molecular bonding sites each play roles in the transformation, proportionately, of combinations of the four qualities (reflected in their molecular-ionic forms). The cortical associative areas, as with the other senses, create an image of tastes based on the same principle of resonant representation. As was true of smell, the sense of taste is not as finely discriminating in us as it is in other mammals; hence, we appreciate its imaging clarity to a lesser degree. To gain a more realistic appreciation of the primordial image of taste, it is helpful to recall that at the uni-cell level, the ability to recognize various molecules and ions that present themselves at the external cell membrane is a crucial survival capacity. At the cell membrane level, it is a compression of touch, taste and smell. As the external senses develop, these three aspects of molecular-ionic contact with the cell membrane differentiate into the three most *ancient* senses.

△ **Touch**—The phrase "sense of touch" is actually a summary expression, as there are several tactile senses in mammals and humans (temperature, pain, light touch/deep touch and vibration). In one-brained creatures, it is closer to a single sense although, even here, there is a degree of specialization in the limb structures that forecasts the highly refined touch of the fingers and hand. In lizards and other reptiles there is also a global touch, mediated by receptors spread over the entire bodily surface. In tunneling, combat and mating, this surface touch (macromolecular contact) leads, via afferent sensory input, to the creation of a whole-body surface image. The fore- and hind-limb touch receptors are afferent sources that serve primarily in the creation of tactile images of surfaces in the outside world (rocks, soil, water, etc.). Touch images formed by the brain can be dramatically illustrated by a simple exercise. If someone were to ask you to close your eyes and they then placed in your outstretched hand a warm, rounded mass of putty with a glass marble imbedded in its center you would gradually form, by pressing, squeezing, etc., an accurate image-in-touch of that object. The image thus formed is a resonant representation of the macromolecular (solid) form placed in your hand.

The types of sensory end-organs for touch are of more simple design in one-brained creatures because their skin lacks hair and the soft, pliable quality and finely controlled capillary circulation that will appear with the second brain. Nonetheless, the mechanoreceptors for touch and vibration transduce the relative solidity and vibratory motions of the external world into a pattern of neural impulses that are proportionate to the physical qualities and vibrations of external surfaces beyond the creature.

In the mechanism of touch, there are no atoms or molecules that will bind to specific sites and no photons that will energize electrons into higher orbits.

In order to resonate with the relatively solid, macromolecular forms and motions of the external world, one-brained creatures had to evolve a variety of relatively solid, interior macromolecular forms that were both *deformable* in a manner proportionate to the solidity of the external object or surface and *sensitive* to the degrees and motions of that deformation.[9] Thus, we see the emergence, from arborized free nerve endings, of a variety of onion-like corpuscles and coiled, vibration-sensitive windings that are responsive, in their structure, to the deformations and vibrations induced by contact with external objects (see illustration 1).

At a molecular level, the physical displacement of the sensitive membrane of the end organ leads to changes in the membrane's ion channels that induce the flow of ions (thought now to be calcium). With this flow, the process of transformation toward a nerve impulse begins. Again, the flow of cations through the channels in the deformed membrane begins a proportionate process that will, with the cortical associative integration of the neural impulses, produce a resonant representation (image) of the external object or surface (illustration 2, page 70).

Memory and Dimensions

Memory and learning can be appropriately spoken of in reference to earlier uni- and multicellular life, but it is a *memory* and *learning* extended over vast periods of time. The molecular membrane and organ adaptations that occur are linked by a feedback principle that is tied to the survival of the whole organism. Thus, an entire species is the evolutionary testing ground and this involves periods immeasurably greater than the life-span of any one member of that species.

When brained life evolved and unique experiential histories appeared, a new and immensely compressed feedback loop began to operate. Learning and memory became coalesced into much briefer time units, with daily events bringing *new* experiences and new experiments in adaptation and modification. While the molecular membrane and organ testings and adaptations continue, they are powerfully influenced by the accelerated feedback deriving from the imaging-motor uniqueness of the brain. An experiential comparative *past* appeared, contained within the individual one-brained being, rather than within the whole species. A tentative *future* appeared, initially built on the power of deception spoken of earlier. Life, through one-brained beings, became temporally three-dimensional.

As the world of solids, liquids, gases and motion/vibrations became imaged by the first brain and this world was explored, via automatic independent motion, the physical three-dimensionality of the external world appeared and was experientially confirmed. The resonant representations deriving from each sense became increasingly interwoven into one experience, primarily via testing and confirmation enabled by movement into the surrounding world.

---

9 This signifies a change in molecular form.

The three-dimensional spatial differentiation of a one-brained being is not well developed, especially as distances increase, but it is an infinite extension beyond the bounding membrane of un-brained, multicellular life. The three dimensions of space, however limited in extent, have appeared, been resonantly represented within a life-form and have been reconciled by a multi-sensed brain interfacing with photonic, ionic, atomic and molecular forms and energies deriving from the dimensionality of the external world.

IN SUM...

The appearance of one-brained beings, in the evolutionary flow of the life of Earth, marks an irrevocable Great Turning. The essence of this turning is the capacity to image the external world, in temporal and spatial dimensions and to move into a world that provides sources of never-ending feedback that will, in turn, enlarge the potential for new images. These new images will eventually explore the world inside the life-form (two-brained beings) and, finally, the world *beyond* outside and inside (in three-brained beings).

ELEMENTAL CONSCIOUSNESS

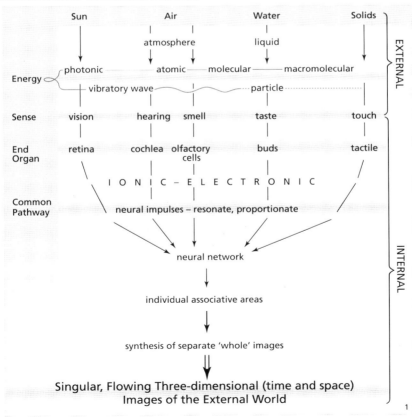

By imaging a portion of each of these energies or forms and then blending these separate images into a flowing whole, the first (core) brain constructed a relatively real and consonant experiential interface with the world around it (illustration 1).

This awareness, of various aspects of the world, at and beyond the body surface, is the most elemental or simple conscious state. It is a substrate attribute which, during the next five hundred million years, will expand and differentiate, turn inward with the mammalian brain and, with the appearance of the human neocortex, turn beyond the inner and outer worlds of the physical body and enter what is a truly abstract state.

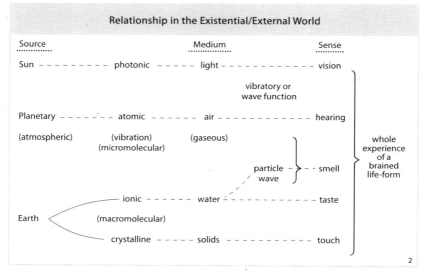

The fundamental principle underlying each of the differentiations of elemental awareness (consciousness) derives from the creation of images or resonant representations of portions of the energies or forms that lie beyond the transformative (sensory) membrane.

SECOND-BRAIN IMAGES

In the case of the mammalian (limbic or second) brain, the boundary surface moves *within* to the various functional interfaces with organs, glands, tissues and portions of the brain itself. Interoceptive input derives primarily from the afferent limb of 1) the muscle spindle and other proprioceptors, 2) the sympathetic and parasympathetic portions of the autonomic nervous system and 3) the neural and neuro-hormone-peptide system centered in the hypothalamic/limbic system. The mammalian brain transduces portions of the photonic, electronic, ionic, vibratory and micromolecular forms and energies that are produced by these internal functions. From these neural impulses, the mammalian brain constructs resonant representations or images of the internal feeling states of the body.

The coalescence of these interoceptive images with the exteroceptive images, deriving from the enhanced external senses of the first brain, form the substrate of what we call the "sense-of-self-other." Mammalian group (family) life becomes firmly anchored-in-image by complimentary gestures, postures, facial expressions, audio/vocal communication, nurturing behaviors and play patterns.

The first brain, in its synthesis of the images deriving from the external senses, is the source of the awareness-of-the-outside-world. The second brain utilizes the (greatly enhanced) full imaging capacity of the first brain and simultaneously fuses this input with that derived from the internal (interoceptive) senses. The result is an entire spectrum-of-awarenesses of the outside world, the inside world and of the two melded into one ~ the *sense-of-self-other*. The sense-of-self-other is, then, a subjective state produced by the functional blending of large neural assemblies, (e.g., the Family Triad of the cingulate gyrus) with the flowing, melded *awarenesses* of the moment.

Observers of mammalian species clearly differentiate the external manifestation of each (and more) of the following: leader, follower, member, mother, father, child-at-play, species group or family, acceptable and unacceptable behaviors, needs, satisfactions, anger, fear, challenge, submission, defeat, sexual interest, curiosity, training, discipline, grief, happiness, warning, protective behaviors.

> ~ Comparative neuroanatomical and neurochemical studies have established quite precise equivalences-in-behavior between two-brained mammals and humans that are associated with multiple neural assemblies of the cingulate gyrus, hippocampus, amygdala and hypothalamus.

> ~ Internal feeling states (emotions), reflected externally in the behaviors noted above, are resultant coalesced images-of-the-moment of self-other. This emotional mentation is a form of cerebration and is characteristically (in humans) manifested in subjective feelings.

On the basis of comparative behaviors, comparative neuroanatomical and neurochemical evidence and the coalescence of images of the first and second brains, there is no objective reason to doubt the reality of awareness-in-feeling among mammals, or their resonance with human feeling as it relates to self, family or species.

At the same time, there is no neuroanatomical or physiological evidence to date that would indicate that mammalian species are aware of these feeling states from a separated, inner perspective.

That evidence appears when the neocortex (the third brain) completes its unique imaging capability – thus establishing a third perspective.

Third-Brain Images

When the pre-frontal cortex completes its cellular differentiation in early Homo species, the third brain (neocortex) can then be spoken of as a functionally separable whole. By "separable" is implied the capacity to function as a relatively singular (independent) and different source of coalesced and multiple images. This relative separation does not alter the total dependence of all neocortical activity on the coordinated function of the first and second brains. When appropriately supported and fed by the earlier evolved brains, the neocortex has the capacity to create and meld images of a totally different nature or order from those created by the first and second brains.[10]

A third level or type of awareness has evolutionarily emerged; one that coalesces images of the world outside and the world inside from a separate viewing place. This will be an awareness that, over time, creates the subjective, experiential singularity inferred by the expression, "I am conscious."

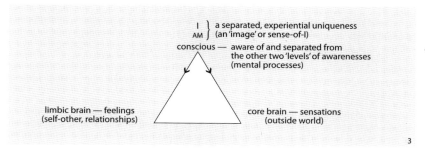

3

Neural Assemblies and Brains

A thin-celled layer of neurons (the germinal neocortex) is present on the outermost surface of the first brain. Even at this early stage of brain evolution, the removal of this outer layer results in the cessation of all self-initiated actions. This is true for mammals as well, but few survive the destruction of this germinal neocortical neuronal assembly.

This impulse-into-action is present in early vertebrate life. It is not a built-in functional expression of any of the master routines or subroutines of the first or second brains. It is not expressed as the result of a coalesced image-associative-patterned motion event (only a *wholed* brain can accomplish this). The elemental cellular coating from which this impulse originates will retain and enormously develop this initiative or purposive thrust-into-action, and become, over hundreds of millions of years, a central feature of the multimillion-celled matrix of the third (neocortical) brain. Illustration 3 outlines the major steps in the process of brain development from the perspective of image completion.

---

10 A rough analogy would be the total dependence of a computer (the third brain) on the steady flow of electricity over power lines and through transformers (the second brain); the electricity, itself, being the result of the proper functioning of a generator (the first brain).

Experiential Dimensions

The third (neocortical) brain adds a third experiential dimension to the imaging capacity of the first (outside world) and second (inside world) brains. Because it has functional capacities and attributes quite unique from the first and second brains it can, to a relative degree, operate by making use of the sensory inputs *and* motor outputs as simultaneous sources of information. By contrast, the awarenesses of first- and second-brained creatures are the information itself. The three experiential dimensions are:

△ First-brained creatures (cold-blooded vertebrates) live, experientially, almost entirely in that outside world; having only the capacities to create images of the world external to their bodily surface, There is no sense of a separated self as there is no inner system of afferent inputs from which an image of self could be created. The resultant awarenesses are, experientially, in that one, external dimension.

△ Second-brained creatures (mammals) add a second experiential dimension by creating resonant representations of the interior functions and states of the body. From the coalesced awarenesses of outside and inside, a two-dimensional experiential world of self-other results.

△ The third brain can experientially stand aside and view the functional expressions (the images) of the first and second brains from a separated perspective (the sense-of-I). From this new perspective, it applies the capacities: to compare, to see analogy, to experiment and, finally, to abstract the principles of how things happen (to 'see' the law), illustration 2.

These capacities/attributes are the direct result of the *new perspective* provided by a different level and hierarchy of awarenesses. The awarenesses are themselves images or resonant representations (compressions or enfoldings, of the first- and second-brain images) now experienced from a separate third perspective.

Thus, human consciousness could be appreciated as being present when a coalescence of three levels or hierarchies of images creates an experiential singularity, relatively separated from sensation (the outside world) and from feeling (the inside world). This singularity (also experienced as the sense-of-I) functions as the source of a global or inclusive state of awareness within which other capacities and attributes can become operant.

Consciousness does not do anything actively from itself, but is the state of perceptual wholeness (small or large) within which capacities for *doing* operate. In this sense, consciousness is akin to a *rheostated* and mobile light source.

- ~ The rheostat analogy could be illustrated by comparing a predawn view of a pond and surrounding trees, with shadows blending from gray to black; with the high noon view in bright colors and sharply-etched features.
- ~ The greater the separation there is between the neocortical coalesced image and the images deriving from the first and second brains, the more inclusive is the consciousness. It could be illustrated in this way.

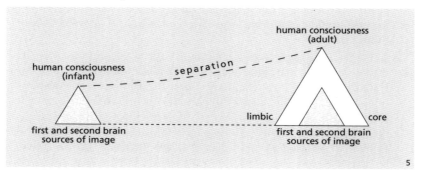

This state of consciousness is thus the qualifying and highly variable, inclusive state of awareness underpinning and permeating all truly human expressions. Following are some examples:

△ A human infant demonstrates the initial defining edge of neocortical coalesced awareness (consciousness) in its attainment of bipedal, independent motion. First-brained images of other humans in the act of walking are the physical models that are imitated. Hosts of second-brained images are processed via the external senses and find enabling resonances within the Family Triad (cingulate gyrus) of nurture, audiovocal communication and play behaviors. The muscle spindle system and other proprioceptors are constant sources of feedback, providing for a real-time, experimental modulation of muscle tensions that build on crossed-extension reflexes and other neural-assembly functional expressions. A large portion of this data, plus that deriving from the afferent input of the autonomic nervous system, vestibular apparatus and basal ganglia, is coalesced by the cerebellum into the image called "the sense-of-balance." Third-brained capacities (with consciousness as the substrate state) blend these first- and second-brained images into a physical (sensory-motor cortex) *understanding* of the laws of bipedal locomotion. This most repetitious process of — the collecting of data ⟶ hypothesis ⟶ experimentation ⟶ verification through failure and success — goes on as the potential capacity for walking undergoes gradual actualization.

In this example, a critical interface in the development of the third brain's multiple levels of awareness is exposed. The infant's consciousness (and sense-of-I) is almost totally absorbed in *wholing* the first- and second-brain images associated with attaining independent bipedal locomotion, as are several of the third brain's fledgling capacities, (i.e., developing and sustaining a focused attention, coordinating the static and dynamic senses of balance). As a result, there is little internal separation of image within the third brain itself and there has not yet coalesced a separated sense-of-I that is able to image the process of locomotion as a functionally separate event. A child masters bipedal locomotion because it has a third brain. While it has begun to demonstrate a sense-of-self-other (deriving from its second brain), it has not yet coalesced a tripartite sense-of-I.

△ A second example concerns the appearance of language. The second brain has, within the cingulate gyrus, a repertoire of audiovocal communications that are elemental forms of sounds-that-stand-for (murmurings, squeals, and grunts, etc.). The separation cry of the infant mammal and the mother's recognition-response will diversify with the evolutionary development of the Family Triad into a wide variety of *sounds-of* nurture, distress, warning, hunger, etc.. All of these are sound images of affective (emotional) states. This process of sounds-that-stand-for becomes a well-established form of sound and image communication long before the brain matures to its wholeness in humans.

The second brain builds on 1) the already extant sound images of affective states fed to it from within itself and 2) the form/energy images of the external world fed to it from the first brain. Because it *stands aside* from both, the third brain experiments (plays) with new, three-sourced images and begins the process of imaging new sounds that stand for forms, motions and energies imaged from the external and internal world. The earliest of these new sounds were likely onomatopoetic or, perhaps, analogs of the sound images of emotional states. In the spoken word, the imaging capacity of the first brain has become melded with one of the distinctive inner imaging and expressive capacities of the second brain by the relational-abstracting capacity of the third brain. This pattern–of bringing aspects of first- and second-brained images into new and completed relationships–is one of the most essential and unique attributes of the third brain.

The pattern just outlined can be seen as a way of understanding the emergence and development of spoken language. The specificity, color and nuance of the individual languages that appear depend, in part, on the geography, the degree of physical isolation, the varieties of wildlife and their sounds and the previously developed (second brain) sounds of nurture, warning, discipline and play. Because each early human grouping lived in unique circumstances with their own unique *histories*, the development of the spoken language also had unique expressive forms and motions. The attribute common to all is the exploratory, creative experimentation undertaken by the third brain's inveterate image-compression capacity. The raw materials are provided by the physical images of the first brain and the biological, processive images of the second brain. In the final segment of this chapter, the imperative, evolutionary appearance of written language, the concept of number, arithmetic principles and mathematics will be briefly addressed from the same perspective of successive image compression.

Language and the other implicate capacities can only demonstrate themselves, however, when a substrate consciousness – the primordial and balanced blending of the functional expression of the first, second and third brains is present. The expression, "the triune brain," first applied by Paul MacLean, reflects, in its own compressed imagery, a similar perspective.

△ As a third example, each of the following words or expressions requires a *consciousness* (or triadic synthesis of fundamental neocortical awareness) in order to have meaning in a human context. Each is also a blending of attributes or capacities which give each word a contextual specificity. The attributes/capacities reflect the variable melding of images deriving from *sensations* ~ as in "fathom" or "thinking it through"; in *feelings* ~ such as "suspect" or "ruminate"; and in *ratiocination* or *logical thinking* ~ such as "cogitate" or "explicate."

As the following words are read, it is useful to 'taste' the shifting nuances in neocortical activity derived from their analogical images and of the resulting sensations and feelings (or first- and second-brain images).

scrutinize – discriminate – evaluate – peruse – suspect – discern – fathom – propose – ruminate – solve – inquire into – take it apart – ascertain – cogitate – postulate – wrangle – equivocate – debate – reason – quibble – rebut – clinch – confound – delineate – dupe – hyperbolize – deceive – distort – assert – dispute – impugn

TIMES AND THE BRAINS

△ First-brain images are resonant representations of a portion of the energies or forms present at or beyond the external surface of the body at the present moment. As such, they reflect the present moment of forms and motions taking place in the external world. Memory and the derivative learning capacities of one-brained creatures are limited to the territorial space and its components. Beyond that, they adapt very slowly, if at all, having fixed master routines and subroutines (which are behaviors deriving from neural assemblies within the first brain) that are triggered by sensory images and/or un-imaged, (unconscious) cyclic, hormonal reactions. Time, for a lizard, is almost entirely a *present* – with a tiny 'tail' of a past.

△ Second-brain images are derived from two sources: enhanced first-brain images of the outside world and images deriving from the states and motions originating within the body. Combined, they are the sources of image that create the sense-of-self-other. The multiple neural assemblies of the second brain (centered in the hippocampus, amygdala, hypothalamus and cingulate gyrus) have densely interwoven feedback circuits connecting the centers that mediate behavioral expression of the *self* (via gamma controlled gesture, posture, carriage, facial expression and vocal tone and via hippocampal-amygdala mediation of elemental affect – i.e., fear and anger) and *self-other* (via the cingulate gyrus – *family triad* of nurturing, audio-vocal communication and play).

One result, of this two-tiered imaging and multi-centered feedback arrangement, is a remarkable expansion of learning capacity and memory. Because it is two-sourced, the second brain evolves the capacity to learn by analogy (comparing *this* to *that* and observing that *this* is like *that*) and, in higher mammals, we find many examples of such learning, e.g., digging with sticks rather than fingers or crushing shells with rocks. While this is a considerable achievement, it lacks the third-dimensional awareness of the capacity of abstraction.

With the great expansion of memory and learning capabilities, the time of mammalian life-forms changes radically. An individual with a unique, past history appears, richly texturing the adaptabilities and experiential *present* life of warm-blooded creatures. The *future*, however, is still almost totally determined by the external forms, states and motions, (i.e., season, climate and motions of other life-forms) and internal forms, (i.e., hormonal and fixed behaviors flowing from the neural centers and their *pasts*).

△ Third-brain images, because they are triune and relatively separated and able to build on the capacities of curiosity, play/exploring and analogical mentation already established by the second brain, can functionally integrate and fuse any and all the first- and second-brain images. This playful exploration and experimentation shows itself early in a child's life – initially in attaining bipedal locomotion (independent motion via the first brain), a bit later in self-assertion (independent *e-motion* via the second brain) and still later in language (reflecting independent mentation via the third brain).

Each of these explicated capacities demonstrates the sudden expansion of the future which the third brain enables. Images of possible futures flow from the separated perspective of the third brain as it looks into the past of the second brain and the present of the first brain. The third brain has the capacity to image in all three times simultaneously (simply another way of expressing the capacity to image how things happen) and abstract the principles (which is another level of compressed image). Mensuration of the future (and past) begins to appear with the concept of number, expanding over time to our present temporal measure of billions of light years.

The Hierarchy of Third-brain Awarenesses

The human third brain, when it demonstrates its complete and successively appearing hierarchy of capacities, unfolds an image, (a step-by-step model) of the scientific method of inquiry. This method of inquiry, which began to take on a describable form at the time of Galileo, is the extraordinary and powerful instrument-of-knowing that it is, because it images in principle or law, the evolutionary form and sequence of the three brains. Brained life explores and selectively validates the nature of the external world, insofar as those physical laws dictate and modify survival. Illustration 6, on the next page, attempts to compress this five-hundred million year event/process, marking each successively more encapsulated awareness as steps in that process.

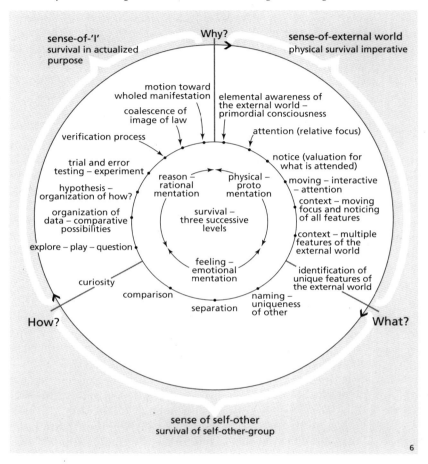

△ Each step introduces a new image or resonant representation, coalescing it with all of the prior steps. For example, in order for a two-brained creature to have the capacity to identify a unique *other*, such as its mate, it must have neurally-based capacities that bring → an elemental awareness → focus → noticing → context → extraction from context, of the unique features, into a near simultaneity-of-image.

△ A brained creature (one-, two- or three-brained) cannot skip steps. It evolves an increasingly simultaneous capacity to meld or blend the successive images. We refer, in using the word "simultaneous," to an experiential (subjective) state of coalesced image. There is still the *process* (the steps) but that process is occurring in such short time intervals that there is rarely (even in humans) an awareness of it. Modern PET and dynamic MRI studies illustrate this point very well. The various and successive parts of the brain which are activated when music is played or when a sentence is spoken are clearly identified on the scan. The person, subjectively, is *not aware* of that process and experiences only the coalescence of image.

△ With the emergence of questioning (which, as compressed image, appears after curiosity and can be understood as a completed *form-image* of curiosity), the unique attributes of the third (neocortical) brain first show themselves. A potentially real and unpredictable future also shows its leading edge.

△ The steps, from data ⟶ exploring ⟶ knowledge ⟶ hypothesis ⟶ testing ⟶ understanding ⟶ wisdom ⟶ through to the coalescence of the *image-of-law*, outline what is usually described as the "scientific method." At the same time, the entire process equally reflects the successive involvement of compressed and integrated images in all uniquely human attainments, i.e., bipedal locomotion, speech, written language, artistic expressions and cultural and scientific principles. The remarkable range of human capacities emerges from the inveterate exploration of possibilities inherent in the unique imaging capacities of the three brains. A taste of this infinite arena can be had by applying the steps in illustration 6: 1) to any first-brain image of the external world, 2) any second-brain images of the interior world, 3) any image that arises from all possible combinations of first- and second-brain images or 4) the uniquely three-dimensional images which flow from the normal functioning of the third brain.

Each human being moves into a uniquely remembered life with feedback loops present at each level of brained function and with imaging capacities that can blend and be trained endlessly further than their initially endowed level.

△ Similarly, each human being has an efferent-controlled musculoskeletal apparatus, which is modulated by all three brains. The confluence (on the anterior horn cells of the spinal cord and brain stem) of efferent influences, deriving from the first, second and third brains, are the simultaneous completion and beginning points of the largest coordinated feedback loop in the body. Action, carried into the external world in whole body movements (first brain), in gesture and facial expression (second brain), or in written mathematical formulae or musical notes (third brain), leads to a change in spatial/temporal orientation, a *new* circumstance and new sources of afferent input to each of the brains. A relative perpetual motion is established.

Consciousness

Human consciousness appears at a particular juncture in the progressive evolutionary unfolding of successively more dense coalesced awarenesses. The earliest manifestation of *awareness* appeared when the first brain created a resonant representation (an image or likeness) of a portion of the exterior forms and energies presented to its bodily surface. This *awareness of* is akin to a uni-directional arrow.

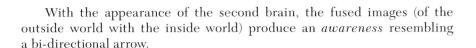

With the appearance of the second brain, the fused images (of the outside world with the inside world) produce an *awareness* resembling a bi-directional arrow.

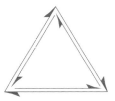

When the third brain creates a *separated* perspective (looking 'down' on the first and second brains), this produces an *awareness* which has the form of an omni-directional triad.

In early childhood years, this human consciousness (or capacity for a global three-dimensional awareness) is neither broad enough nor inclusive enough to coalesce a clearly experienced *sense-of-I* (a separated awareness of oneself as a thinking, feeling, sensate/moving individuality). The transition to the full sense-of-I could be represented in this way:

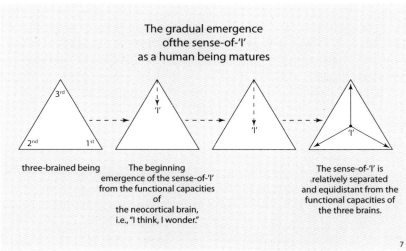

The gradual emergence of the sense-of-'I' as a human being matures

three-brained being | The beginning emergence of the sense-of-'I' from the functional capacities of the neocortical brain, i.e., "I think, I wonder." | | The sense-of-'I' is relatively separated and equidistant from the functional capacities of the three brains.

The emergent sense of individuality ('I'), when in a balanced relationship with each of the brains, is able to initiate a motion into and through any one of the three. The initiation of motion, or thrust into action, is the fully evolved capacity initially seen in one-brained creatures.

In chapter 4 (page 113), we have detailed the presence of the thin cell layer (primordial neocortex) overlaying the first brain. This elemental neocortical grouping of neurons (immensely distant from a 'brain' at this time) provides the thrust-into-action for reptilian life. Without it, nothing happens from within the creature. Its master routines and subroutines can be evoked, from *outside* by a particular stimulus, (i.e., dropping it in water, placing food in its mouth), but, as soon as the display pattern, organized by the portion of the first brain which has been stimulated, is completed, the creature comes to a full *stop* (ceases all external motion).

This elemental cell layer (which eventually becomes the completed third brain) undergoes evolutionary differentiation, maintaining the capacity to initiate action (or motion) in all newly appearing, cerebral developments of the second and third brain.

Most importantly this outer, elemental cell layer becomes, with the maturation of Homo sapiens, the core of his sense-of-I, the thrust-into-action which:

questions ⟶ explores ⟶ takes apart ⟶ gathers data ⟶
forms hypotheses ⟶ constructs and conducts experiments.

If the abstracted principle proves, in time, to be invalid or incomplete, the thrust-into-action drives him back to his original question.

This *scientific methodology* is just as applicable, as mentioned earlier, to the unfolding capacities of the third brain of an infant when it undertakes to walk independently and, later, when it undertakes to talk, write, read, do mathematics, ride a bike, play a musical instrument or ponder the nature of consciousness.

The illustrations on the following two pages, show the expanding and deepening arenas of awarenesses, beginning from the simple but real image of an early one-brained creature and ending in the coalescence of the awarenesses of all three brains in a mature adult human.

For illustrative purposes, the appearance and differentiation of the first, second and third brains are sharply demarcated. The reality is otherwise because neural assemblies, which will become the higher brains, are present in the first brain and there is a gradual blending, through evolutionary time, of the interfaces of and between the brains. Figure 8 shows this differentiation and illustrates these points.

Illustrations 8 and 9 attempt to create a geometric image of human consciousness as a variable, expandable state of global (inclusive) *awareness*.

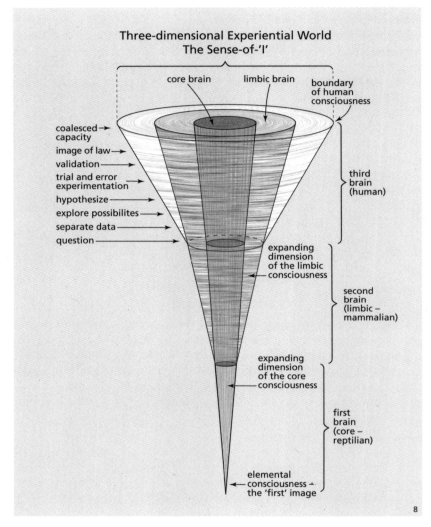

Within the bowl of expandable, global *awareness* (consciousness), the capacities outlined in illustration 6 will be displayed. The capacities (steps in illustration 6) are actually three-dimensional – all the steps being present but tightly linked to the first and second brains. With human maturation and exercise of the individual capacities, an expansion is undergone, parallel with the expansion of consciousness (illustration 10 details this point).

This three-dimensional illustration cannot reflect the dynamic sharing and interaction that is a constancy of brained function. The primary axonal and associative axonal-dendritic-neurotransmitter feedback loops and the em field synchronicities are unapproachable with this form. An attempt can be made in this direction by trying to image mentally a blending of illustration 6, on page 78, and illustration 11, on page 84.

Neural assemblies provide organized patterns of behavior but are not yet capable of creating wholed images and developing variable, associative sensory-motor patterns of expression.

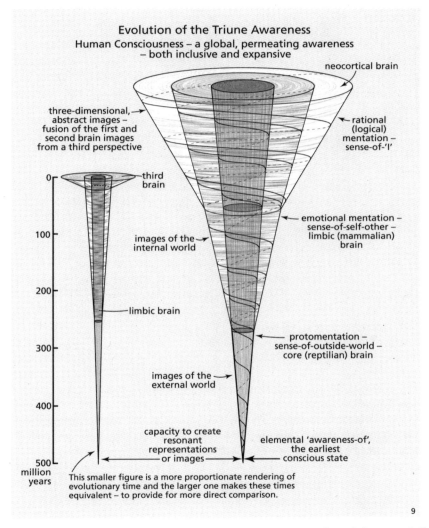

A different way of viewing the gradual coalescence of modules into fully functional brains is illustrated above. The earliest neural assemblies (ganglia) are thought to have appeared approximately six-hundred million years ago. The neural assemblies (light gray) gradually become complexified into modules (darker gray) of what will become the respective brain.

The Material Nature of Consciousness, Images and Attention

From the perspective put forward thus far, there are still questions concerning the nature of material energies and forms which are involved in the brain's creation of images, the various states of consciousness and the unique phenomenon of attention.

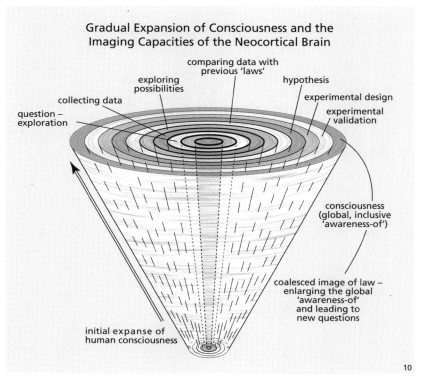

Consciousness

We posit that consciousness (whether of one-, two- or three-brained beings) is based upon electromagnetic (em) field phenomena that are produced by the billions of brain cells. As MacFadden notes,

> "All electrical phenomena involve the generation of electromagnetic (em) fields. Neurons have massive voltage differences across their cell membrane and voltage is, of course, a measure of the em field's gradient. However, this field will extend beyond the neuron. The fields generated by one hundred billion neurons must overlap and superimpose, to generate an extraordinarily complex em field inside our brain."[11]

---

11 Johnjoe MacFadden, *Quantum Evolution*, p 295.

Em fields interpenetrate each other without interference and this makes possible the registration of multiple overlapping fields that have their origin in widely separated groupings (modules) of brain cells. Varying combinations of modular em fields form the basis of different conscious states.

From this perspective, consciousness, in its 'pure' or most elemental state, has no specific content (there are no images imbedded or appearing within the awareness). It is simply a state of awareness, not of 'awareness-of anything'. As difficult as this elemental state is to describe in words, it has been approached, in metaphorical descriptions, by many contemplative traditions (in the author's acquaintance, this includes Buddhist, Christian and Sufi).

Images

The images which derive from the wide variety of sensory and associative inputs (ionic wave impulses) to the various brain modules are 'projected' on or within the 'screen' (or contextual background) formed by the fields generated by multiple modules of brain function. In this action, there is a complex and variable blending of images from each of the three brains — outer world images of the first brain (external sensations), inner world images of the second brain (feelings) and abstract images of the third brain (images of spoken and written language and other types of compounded abstractions, e.g., concepts of number, geometrical forms, personal and social ideas, of metaphorical expressions in poetry and epic myth and music, dance and drama).

Attention

Multiple, constantly changing images are produced within, or on, the screen of consciousness and this multiplicity raises a question as to which images become focused upon, at any given moment or during any given event. Attention is the word that is most frequently applied to this discriminating power. We posit that light waves (photons) are the carrier of a triadic power to focus, to separate and to see relationships.[12] A metaphorical expression of this would be to say that attention is like a light beam which is automatically or intentionally directed onto the multi-leveled forms (three-brained images) that appear on the 'stage' or background of elemental awareness (consciousness). Many myths and allegorical tales can be understood as metaphorical representations of the relationship between images, consciousness and attention.[13]

12 While it is known that living cells emit very low frequency photons under a variety of conditions, the specific functions connected to their emissions are not known. Present day neurophysiological research has not investigated this phenomenon as it may apply to brain function.

13 A familiar Sufi favorite is this:
    One night Nasrudin was looking desperately under the street lamp. His neighbors saw him and asked him what he lost. He answered, "My key!" So, his neighbors started to look for it as well, all around the street lamp. After one hour, nobody found anything! So finally they asked him, "Do you remember where you lost your key?" Nasrudin answered, "Yes, it must be somewhere there in the dark, far from the street lamp." They asked him; "If you lost it there, why are you looking for it here under the street lamp?" Nasrudin, "Because under the street lamp I can see!"

For example, the automatically directed attention refers to the use of this power by the instinctive/moving-center. For the majority of humans, physical survival is the most potent directive of the attention when the images registered are interpreted as threats to the body. Attention is also automatically directed as a result of the multitude of early life relational experiences that qualify the meanings of images. Gurdjieff refers to this as the process of Itoklanoz:[14] the imposition, via DNA, parents, family, community and culture, of values and perspectives over which the individual has little or no control.

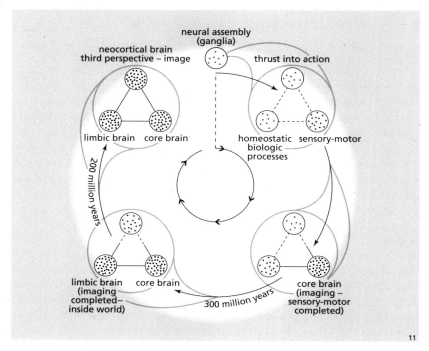

Intentionally directed attention implies the presence of a choice for an individual; a situation where alternatives are recognized and a decision is made as to where the attention is to be placed. The relationship between images, consciousness and automatic or directed attention is illustrated in triadic form above.

---

14 Gurdjieff, *Beelzebub's Tales*, pp 131, 438.

Will

The Will, when understood as a truly independent source of *decisioning* (standing independent of Itoklanoz), is higher (in potency) than impulse, image, consciousness or attention. We assign the potency of the Will[15] to the em force itself. The following summarizes these differentiations:

neural impulses	ionic waves
images	organized patterns of ionic wave forms
consciousness	complex overlapping em fields
attention	photons (light waves)
Will	em force itself

While this arrangement of em phenomena is quite simplified, it does provide an outline of fundamental cerebral processes and capacities that is consistent with subjective experience and with some recently appearing neurophysiological findings. These will be discussed in the next chapter.

---

15 The Will also includes the instinctive forces that are the substrate of life itself.

CHAPTER 3 PAGE 60 ENDNOTES
  I Sir Arthur Eddington, *The Nature of the Physical World*, P 332.
  II Niels Bohr, *The Philosophical Writings of Niels Bohr*, Volume 2, P 73.
  III Renee Weber, *Dialogues with Scientists and Sages*, P 237, quoting the Dalai Lama.

Man—A Three-brained Being

"In every three-brained being in general, irrespective of the place of his arising and the form of his exterior coating, there can be crystallized data for three independent kinds of being-mentation, the totality of the engendered results of which expresses the gradation of his Reason."[I]

"I find it necessary to repeat that the 'active-mentation' in a being and the useful results of such active mentation are in reality actualized exclusively only with the equal-degree functionings of all his three localizations of the results spiritualized in his presence, called 'thinking-center,' 'feeling-center,' and 'moving-motor-center.'"[II]

Preface to Chapter 4

Words, phrases, sentences and symbols, necessarily gain their initial meanings via our thinking-center (our intellectual or third brain). Too often this level of meaning remains isolated in the abstract world of ideas and concepts; never confronting, or being confronted by, the equally important centers of feeling mentation (emotional/relational) and moving mentation (where all practical manifestations are given a form).

Less often—the ideas and concepts derived from the functioning of the thinking-center may be incorporated into physical manifestation, via inventions and other utilitarian enterprises, with the results having powerful influences on man's life, (e.g., the cotton gin, the steam and internal combustion engines, the dynamo). As history confirms, these thinking- and moving-center developments have most often occurred without the equal participation of the feeling-center (where personal, family and community relationships are associatively explored and expressed).

Put more simply—man, in recent centuries, has rarely considered the consequences, in terms of human relationships, of the utilitarian applications of his 'thinking'. The destructive influences of the industrial revolution on family and community life are one example, as are the more recent deleterious influences of television and computer games on the normal brain development of young children. In these examples, it is the *absence* of "equal-degree functioning of all his three localizations" (or brains) which is emphasized. The *balanced* participation of all three 'brains' is intrinsic to the application of the ideas and concepts taken up in this chapter.

It is one thing to *write* or *talk* about efforts to direct the attention, to self-remember, to establish a separated 'presence' to the world of images or to make a conscious effort to 'follow the breath'. It is another thing, altogether, to make the effort to *do* it. The discussions undertaken in this chapter will result in nothing but vaporous ideas and 'a-thinkings' if concerted effort is not made to apply the ideas to one's own subjective, inner experience. However, when this type of personal effort *is* made, a process of confrontation and possible verification is set in motion. One begins, with this three-brained effort, to experience the requirements which are prerequisite to the process of "active mentation."

"You were asking about pure awareness. Even there, there are relative and ultimate stages of empty awareness. Right now you can be aware that you are aware. Without particularly attending to any of the objects of awareness, you can simply sit there and be immediately aware of being aware. Can you not? You don't have to understand that by inference, do you? What image came to mind when you were simply focusing on being aware?"[III]

"Truth cannot be cut up into pieces and arranged in a system. The words can only be used as a figure of speech."[IV]

"By becoming attached to names and forms, not realizing that they have no more basis than the activities of the mind itself, error arises and the way to emancipation is blocked."[V]

"... not one of you has noticed that *you do not remember yourselves*. You do not feel *yourselves*; you are not conscious of *yourselves*."[VI]

CHAPTER 4
THE DIGESTION OF FOOD, AIR AND IMPRESSIONS: A METAPHOR FOR HUMAN TRANSFORMATION

INTRODUCTION
A Metaphorical View of Reality

Man, as a three-brained being, lives in three worlds: the *outer* (the material universe of stars, planets, bodies and energies), the *inner* (the world of subjectively experienced feelings, values and relationships) and the *abstract* (the world of non-mass-based language, concepts, purposes and descriptive laws). These worlds (or levels within the Ray of Creation)[1] are, in their natures, so different from each other that any effort to produce a single description of *reality* that accurately integrates all three is bound to be limited or to fail in certain respects.[2] The question of the nature of reality is an extremely ancient one and is reflected in both the oldest and the most recent of man's efforts to speak about it.[3] In the end, the language of metaphor or allegory has proven to be the most enduring approach. This is seen in the persisting significance and value given to epic poetry, allegorical tales, parables, bardic lore and other various and resonant art forms. In addition, the most long-lasting and

---

1 Ouspensky, *In Search*, p 174.
2 For example, man is presently confounded by the contradictions inherent in a view of the cosmos that must include the macro-physical world of galaxies, stars, planets and living creatures and the quantum world of wave/particle dualities. Separate from both of them lies the reality of consciousness, values and purposes.
3 Indeed, it could be understood that the questioning of reality is a natural, emergent property of the third brain.

influential of scientific considerations of reality (from Aristotle and Plato to Einstein, Bohr and Schrödinger) are also marked by a pervasive dependence on metaphorical language.

Gurdjieff chose to speak of this approach as "Podobnisirnian" or "Similnisirnian" ("allegorical")[4] and the various aspects of Fourth Way work make constant use of metaphorical expressions in order to link the three worlds. It is especially important to keep this in mind when he speaks in a direct, factual manner—as is more often the case with Ouspensky's *In Search* than it is with *Beelzebub's Tales*. We have to remember that he is *always* speaking with reference to all three worlds and thus, our best efforts to actively mentate (the blending or "equal-degree functioning" of all three brains) are required.

> "I find it necessary to repeat that the 'active mentation' in a being and the useful results of such active mentation are in reality actualized exclusively only with the equal-degree functionings of all his three localizations of the results spiritualized in his presence, called 'thinking-center,' 'feeling-center,' and 'moving-motor-center.'"[5]

Nowhere is the breadth and depth of understanding more true than with his presentations concerning the digestion/transformation of food, air and impressions.[6] If we are not acutely attentive, we will overemphasize the approach to one of these worlds and miss the metaphorical references to the other two.

In Ouspensky's *In Search*,[7] Gurdjieff uses the words "digestion" and "transformation" when he speaks about the assimilation of the three foods. By contrast, in *Beelzebub's Tales*,[8] the words "transformation," "transmute" and "evolution" are applied to the *process of the assimilation* of the three "being foods." The difference in terminology emphasizes the more factual presentation of *In Search*, in contrast to metaphorical presentation of *The Tales*, which permits a more broad and subtle appreciation of the cosmic dimensions of the process. This difference is reflected in the following quotations:

> "All the fine substances necessary for the growth and feeding of the higher bodies must be produced within the physical organism, and the physical organism is able to produce them provided the human factory is working properly and economically."[9]

> "And if now, my boy, you satisfactorily grasp the succession of the process of transformation of cosmic substances by means of being-apparatuses, into which these cosmic substances enter as first being-food, then at the same time, you will approximately understand everything concerning the chief particularity of the sacred law of

---

4 Gurdjieff, *Beelzebub's Tales*, pp 738-39.
5 Ibid., p 1172.
6 The more factual presentation is in *In Search*, pp 179-93; the more metaphorical, in *Beelzebub's Tales*, pp 785-93.
7 Ouspensky, *In Search*, pp 179-93.
8 Gurdjieff, *Beelzebub's Tales*, pp 785-93.
9 Ouspensky, *In Search*, p 180.

Heptaparaparshinokh as well as the processes of evolution and involution of the other higher being-foods."[10]

It is also useful to note the differences in the common and metaphorical meanings of digestion, transformation, transmutation and evolution. With digestion (beyond the common meaning of the material 'taking apart' or of the reduction to constituent parts), there are also the contextual meanings of "taking in; mental reception or assimilation" and "to tolerate patiently; to endure."[11] The breadth of common and metaphorical meanings of transformation, transmutation and evolution is quite different than digestion, with the emphasis being on "change of form" (whether in physical, emotional or thought 'form') and on an "upward or more refined movement." Also to be kept in mind is Gurdjieff's understanding and application of the word "evolution," which infers a quite different process than the more well-known Darwinian usage infers.

To varying degrees, all of the aforementioned meanings can be selectively applied to his discussion of the three foods. By noting that the origin and overlapping octavic digestion of the three foods (by 'hydrogen' number)[12] extends through all three cosmic octaves (Absolute–Sun; Sun–Earth; Earth–Moon),[13] he emphasizes that each three-brained being functions in three separate but contiguous–overlapping worlds. To discuss such a comprehensive view requires a language rich in metaphor.

Metaphor and the Octave

Each note (DO–RE–MI–FA–SOL–LA–SI) in an enneagramatic, evolutional octave has specific qualities and attributes that reflect the *functions* of that note within the octave. Therefore, there will always be a resonance or similitude between all DOs, all REs, all MIs, etc.. Since there are many different kinds of evolutional octaves within and between the cosmic octaves of: Absolute–Sun, Sun–Earth and Earth–Moon (illustration 1), the qualities and attributes that we will ascribe to each note have to be understood in a most *metaphorical* sense. Each of the words we have chosen is a compromise that is intended to be interpreted in both a literal and Similnisirnian manner.

DO — decision; purpose, goal or aim; resonance with all notes

RE — first entry into the arena of action; initial assessment; defining the task

MI — production of 'elementals', in which the aim is foreshadowed

MI–FA — outer meets inner; new energy source; resistance defined

FA — the *body* is entered; maintenance and growth energies are established

---

10 Gurdjieff, *Beelzebub's Tales*, p 786.
11 *Funk and Wagnalls Standard College Dictionary*
12 Gurdjieff defines levels of material vibration through hydrogen numbers H_{3072} to H_6. See Buzzell, *Perspectives on Beelzebub's Tales*, chapter 9, "Gurdjieff's 'hydrogens'," pp 115-49 for a more thorough exploration of the categories of material vibrations.
13 Ouspensky, *In Search*, p 174.

Man—A Three-brained Being

SOL — new basis of energy; defining of inner/outer relationships
SOL–LA — hazardous 'inner' passage through the Harnel-Aoot
LA — elemental form or pattern emerges
SI — freedom from the past; blending of outer and inner
SI–DO — creative potentiality into the future

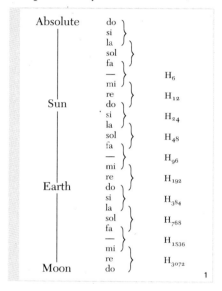

The Role of Directed Attention

Of all the lawful processes that we must come to understand and in which we must become able to be active participants, in Gurdjieff's view, none is more essential than the process of the digestion or the transformation of physical food, air and impressions. All possibilities of self-evolution are pinioned on it and the whole of Work can be understood as a "perfect synthesis"[14] of it.

Gurdjieff delves into the interstices of this process in considerable detail, both in *The Tales* and in Ouspensky's record *In Search*, using, as a lawful model, the automatic digestion of food. While the process retains the same enneagramatic form in both the digestion of air and impressions, a fundamental difference lies in the requirement that *directed attention* be a primary participant. How that can *begin* to take place is explored in this chapter.

The Three Foods

"The human organism receives three kinds of food:
1. The ordinary food we eat
2. The air we breathe
3. Our impressions.

---

14 Ouspensky, *In Search*, p 293.

"It is not difficult to agree that air is a kind of food for the organism. But in what way impressions can be food may appear, at first, difficult to understand. We must however remember that, with every external impression, whether it takes the form of sound, or vision, or smell, we receive from outside a certain amount of energy, a certain number of vibrations; this energy which enters the organism from outside is food. ...

[and]

...The flow of impressions coming to us from outside is like a driving belt communicating motion to us. The principal motor for us is nature, the surrounding world. Nature transmits to us through our impressions the energy by which we live and move and have our being."[15]

The notion that man ingests three categories of food is quite new to the Western world. References to air and impressions, as necessary for the higher spiritual functions of man, are made in many spiritual traditions (especially those of the East) but Gurdjieff is the first to speak of them as the three primary sources of energy for the physical, emotional and intellectual life, as well as them having unique relationships to time, (i.e., man can live for many days without physical food; he can live for approximately four minutes without air; he is instantly dead if he cannot take in impressions).

Physical Food (H_{768})

Gurdjieff includes the flesh and fluids of previously living plants and animals (all of those that the stomach and intestines can digest) in his category of "food for man" (H_{768}). When we recall the different cultures and the varied climatic conditions obtaining on the earth over many thousands of years, this category is seen to be very large. As food for man, it must provide sufficient proteins, fats and carbohydrates (to be broken down into the essential amino acids, glycerol, fatty acids and simple sugars) for the growth and maintenance of the body.

"Inner growth, the growth of the inner bodies of man, the astral [Kesdjan], the mental [Higher Being], and so on, is a material process completely analogous to the growth of the physical body."[16]

The digestion of physical food is, then, an octavic model for the digestion of air and of impressions. We have developed our perspective by examining in some detail current physiological understandings of the digestion of physical food. Those steps have been placed on the enneagramatic model as presented by Ouspensky[17] and on this, we have identified a number of essential principles and events that characterize the digestive process and that will eventually be applied to the digestion of air and of impressions.

15 Ouspensky, *In Search*, P 181.
16 Ibid., P 180.
17 Ibid., PP 182-88 and 377.

Man—A Three-brained Being

The classical form of the three-octave enneagram is placed below for reference (figure 2)[18] – with the triadic form following (figure 3).[19]

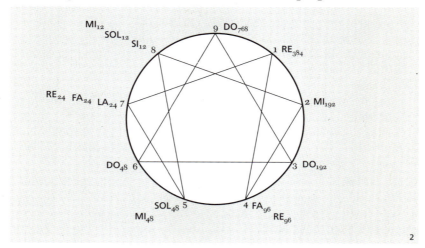

2

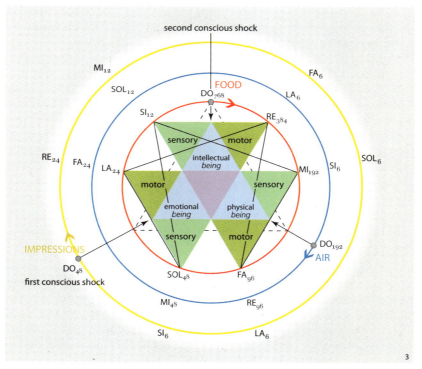

3

18 Ouspensky, *In Search*, p 377.
19 "Physical," "emotional," "intellectual" are used interchangeably with "motor-moving," "feeling" and "thinking." See Buzzell, *Explorations*, "The Function of Emotion," pp 18-19.

DO — The process of digestion begins when food is placed in the mouth. There is, then, a chewing and mixing, which requires energy expenditure via the muscles of mastication and the secretion of a specialized muco-protein/water mixture that requires cellular energy to manufacture, as well as smooth muscle contractions to pump the mucous from its glandular origin to the mouth itself. This mucous is a loss (via elimination); an expenditure of organized forms and energies that are not retrieved, just as the burning of ATP provides energy for the action of chewing but is ultimately lost. Material vibrations of a much higher level (higher than the physical energies expended in chewing) must be supplied from within and secreted into a space that is outside the body (the oral cavity). The lining cells of the gastro-intestinal tract are like the skin in that they both mark the boundary or interface between what is outside the body and what is inside. In the instance of physical food, the outside is the interior of the gastrointestinal tract (mouth–stomach–intestine), which is a tube that extends from the mouth to the anus but whose contents lie *outside* of the physical body.

RE — When a certain consistency has been reached, the bolus of chewed food is swallowed (taken further within but still *outside* of the body). The upper esophagus, the muscular tube joining the mouth to the stomach, is under voluntary, or conscious, control (largely as a protective measure – we can still bring up and get rid of small bones, particles, etc., if need be) whereas, the lower esophagus is under automatic control – meaning that an elaborate but unconscious neural process guides the action of swallowing beyond the upper esophagus.

The food bolus, a textured, mucousy mix of small but still macromolecular food, is brought into the highly acidic milieu of the stomach. Here, the mixing/churning continues to a degree, while the acidic environment provides an optimized circumstance for a group of enzymes to begin the work of taking apart or *unbonding* the macromolecular protein food particles. The result is a mixture of long molecular chains of amino acids (polypeptides), long chains of fatty molecules, a variety of simple and complex sugars and many dissolved and undissolved salts, mineral compounds and ions.

MI — From here, the mix is slowly propelled into the small intestine, where a dramatically different, alkaline milieu is induced and into which a host of enzymes are secreted. The many types of enzymes (lipases for fats, glucose phosphatases for sugar and peptidases for the protein fragments) unbond or separate the macromolecular foods at certain linkage sites, producing the amino acids, fatty acids, glycerol and glucose that can be actively absorbed across the cell membrane and enter the blood and lymph vessels. In the actions that take place in the stomach and small intestine, there is a large expenditure of refined energies and forms. Each of the enzymes is individually crafted within the cells lining the villi of the gastrointestinal tube and is secreted into the external space of the intestine. All of the many thousands of specialized molecules are degraded and eliminated after performing their unbonding functions.

MI – FA — It is only at the point of absorption into the blood and lymph that we can truly say that the food has entered the body. To get to this point, the body has had to expend considerable amounts of highly coordinated energy in muscular contractions and in the synthesis of specialized molecules. Further, the body must move and control the flow of a large portion of the blood, bringing it from the skeletal muscle mass to the vessels of the gastrointestinal tract and, thence, to the liver. This intricately interwoven cycle is repeated each time food is brought to the mouth. It is useful to outline the cycle to this point:

- DO — physical food (macromolecular, 'solid' forms) is introduced into the mouth
    - ~ chewing and mixing with mucous (smaller macromolecules and slight absorption of glucose)
    - ~ swallowing (more interior but still exterior to the body)
- RE — mixing in the liquid acid environment of the stomach; the presence of protein enzymes – the beginning separation of micromolecules
- MI — mixing and moving into the alkaline environment of the small intestine
    - ~ presence of many enzymes of three categories (protein ⟶ amino acid; carbohydrate ⟶ glucose; fats ⟶ fatty acids and glycerol) production of micromolecules, molecules and ions
- MI–FA — entry into the body (active absorption across the cell membrane and into the lymph vessels and bloodstream)

We have come, in Gurdjieff's terms, to the MI–FA interval (which in *The Tales* is called the "mechano-coinciding-Mdnel-In"). It is here that air *enters* and enables the octave of our first-being food to continue the digestive process.

AIR AS FOOD

"Air" (H_{192}), as Gurdjieff applies the word in the context of food, requires different considerations. The importance of oxygen, as a 'food', is well established and has been thoroughly investigated over the past fifty years. Until recently, investigators had given little attention to other substances carried by air. Ionic (charged) forms of various atoms and micromolecular structures, that include pheromones[20] and hormones of considerable variety, have been identified as being absorbed into the body via the lungs, where they function as activators of biological processes.

The pressure of air and its water content (humidity) are also factors that have to be considered as 'parts' of the air, but which do not appear to be 'food' in Gurdjieff's terms. Also, nitrogen and carbon dioxide make up a considerable majority of the atoms and molecules contained in air but, since they are

---

20 These are hormones secreted by plants and animals into the air.

not absorbed into the body, they are not considered part of the food of air. Expiration or breathing out contains, in addition, a quantity of CO_2 *eliminated* by the body.

Just as macromolecular physical food must be taken apart (unbonded) to reach a level that can provide energies and forms that the body can absorb and use, air must go through a similar unbonding process. With respect to air, the unbonding process clearly applies to oxygen, which as O_2 is in a bonded diatomic form (two oxygen atoms bonded together) and must have this bond broken (or opened) in order for the resultant ionic oxygen atom (O^-) to function as an energy source.

Reference to illustration 3 will be helpful at this point. The passage from DO_{192} to RE_{96} of air and of MI_{192} to FA_{96} of physical food begins to demonstrate the wide-ranging power of this 'second' food, for it is the ionic form of the oxygen atom that supplies the electronic energy for a host of essential biological processes. Hormones, enzymes, vitamins, proteins, neuro-transmitters, intracellular production of ATP and all neural transmission require electron (–) and/or proton (+) transfers as their activating energy, and ionic oxygen (O^-) is the primary power source driving these elemental processes. There are no other molecular or atomic constituents of the air that are known to serve as sources of energy or forms (food) for the physical body. It is our contention, however, that other, *non-mass-based* 'components' of air are of critical importance to its further digestion. These components will be considered further on.

MI_{48} *and* SOL_{48}

The category H_{48} is comprised of ionic waveforms, which is how neural (nerve) impulses are transmitted. All sensory, associative and motor transmission within the nervous system is of this nature. SOL_{48} represents the neural impulses that mediate the external senses, the first-brain associative cortex and the motor innervation of the skeletal muscles. MI_{48} represents the neural impulses that mediate the internal senses, the gamma system, the autonomic nervous system and the limbic (second-brain) associative cortical activity.

IMPRESSIONS (H_{48}) AS FOOD FOR ALL THREE BRAINS

Each brain creates images from the neural impulses (DO–MI–SOL_{48}) that flow into it (fig. 5, page 102). In the instance of physical food, the elements (carbon, hydrogen, nitrogen, oxygen, sulphur, sodium, etc.,) and the multiple patterns of their chemically bonded combinations, determine the form and sequence of a carrot, bread or any other food. In the instance of an impression, there is an analogous patterned bonding of its elements but its 'elements' are drawn from the forms and energies of the external, internal and abstract worlds.

Each of the sensory end organs of the five external senses forms an interface with certain of the energies and forms of the outside world. The end-organ interfaces and the corresponding energies or forms are outlined on illustration 4 on the following page.

Sense	Receptor–Transformer	Energy/Form
Vision	retinal cells of the eye	reflected array of photons (light)
Hearing	Organ of Corti in the ear	molecular–atomic–ionic vibratory waves
Smell	receptor cells lining the upper nasal chamber	molecular form from air
Tactile Sense (touch)	receptor cells in the skin and mucous membranes	macromolecular form

4

From this perspective, the external senses are arenas-of-contact with the entire range of forms and energies present in the outside, material world—from photonic (electromagnetic radiation), to vibratory atomic-ionic waves, to atomic-ionic, to molecular and macromolecular forms.

Each sense transforms a portion of the varied external forms and energies into a common energy substrate, which is the neural impulse (an ionic wave). The patterning (the form and sequence) of the resultant dense array of neural impulses is transported into the respective sensory center in the brain where complex associative interactions produce an image or resonant representation of the forms and energies of the outside world. These wholed images are the food of impressions; equivalent to, and resonant with, the raw carrot or bread of the first 'being' food.

All brains (first, second and third) pursue, or hunt for, *meaning* and each brain responds to, or expresses, that meaning in the context of survival.

△ The first brain pursues meanings of the images of the external world. Its responses are driven by the imperative toward physical survival. 'Foods' for this brain are the external world images and their subsequent significances and meanings.

△ The second brain pursues the meanings of feeling (inner-world) images and develops responses that are elementally driven by the imperative of *social* (or interactional) survival. Foods for this brain are relational images (feeling impressions) and their self-other meanings.

△ The third brain pursues (or hunts for) meanings and the expression of those meanings in the world of abstractions (language, number, concepts, etc.). Foods for this brain are the elemental images that underpin language, number, concept and their subsequent combinations and elaborations. Survival, with respect to the third brain, concerns the perpetuity of the products of the abstracting capacities (e.g., in literature, spoken words, scientific formulae, artistic and spiritual achievements).

It may seem strange to describe the end product of sensory processing as a food. This is made clear, however, when we contrast the bodies (physical, Kesdjan and Higher Being-body), which are to be fed by their respective foods. For example, the cellular structure of our planetary body is fed by the micromolecular amino acids, fats and sugars. Our brains, in the cellular sense, are fed by this same array of micromolecules. However, in their functioning as instruments of mentation, they require a very different array of material/ vibrations and this is provided by the images or resonant representations created by each of them:[21]

△ The first brain receives data (which is food) that is almost exclusively about the world at and beyond the boundary of the planetary body (light, sound, chemicals, odors and solids/liquids).

△ The second brain (characteristic of all mammals) receives data/food from the first brain and simultaneously receives enormous input reflecting, in feeling images, the dynamic processes taking place within the planetary body itself.[22] It is this coalesced input which is the substrate for the sense-of-self-other which sharply differentiates the level of mentation of mammals from that of cold-blooded creatures (whose protomentation[23] is derived almost exclusively from a first-brain sense-of-the-outside world).

△ The third brain has three sources of data/food:
~ first-brain images of the outside world (the sense-of-the-outside world)
~ second-brain images of the inside world; both for itself and as coalesced with the images of the first brain (the sense-of-self-other)
~ third-brain images which are the abstract creations that underpin language, concepts of number, art, law, beauty, etc.. It is an independent and singular perspective and a viewing place of the data (images) deriving from the first and second brains. It is this combined afferent input, seen from a singular but third perspective which, when combined with the powers of abstraction, creates the elemental sense-of-I characteristic of three-brained beings.

IN SUM ...

Food, in a process of first, second or third brain mentation, follows the same octavic form and sequence in its digestive process. Cascades of neural impulses activate and associatively move through the sensory processing centers of each brain. From this delicately orchestrated array of ionic-electronic 'motions', an image or resonant representation (an impression) results. These impressions are food for a brain (H_{48}, 24, 12 and 6; these are Gurdjieff's psychic/spiritual 'hydrogens'). Note the triads of $DO_{48}-MI_{48}-SOL_{48}$ and $RE_{24}-FA_{24}-LA_{24}$ and $MI_{12}-SOL_{12}-SI_{12}$ in illustration 5 on the following page.

---

21 See chapter 3, with the heading "The Material Nature of Consciousness, Images and Attention" in this volume, PP 84-87.
22 See chapter 2, "The Triune Brain" in this volume,
23 MacLean, *The Triune Brain in Evolution*, P 12. Also see chapter 2, P 49 and the glossary.

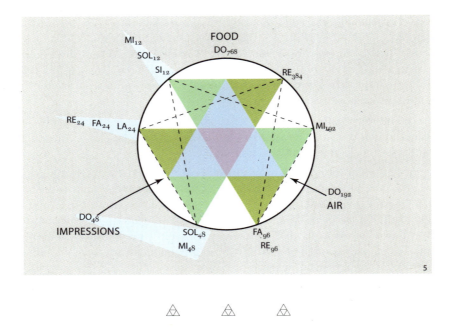

Gurdjieff's Metaphor of 'Food'

Food, by definition, is any substance that, when ingested and digested, contributes to the growth and maintenance of the body. The words "food," "ingested/digested," "substance" and "body" have to be understood metaphorically if we are to comprehend his application of them to air and impressions. "Substance" refers to any material/vibration in the 'hydrogen' categories which can perform a function in the body. "Ingested" refers to the process of absorption or transformation (into another form) by which a substance is taken into the body. "Body" is used in a very metaphorical way here; it refers to a unified, highly organized and balanced state which can function (with sensory, associative and motor capacities) relatively independently, as a *one*; a *whole*.

The air octave, in Gurdjieff's terms, includes all of the hydrogens from H_{192} to H_6 that carry out some essential function in the feeling (emotional) life of man. This would include the second-brain impulses toward nurture, respectful communication and playful behaviors as well as 'higher' impulses and images related to Faith, Hope, Love and Conscience. The 'body' which is fed this food has its substrate materiality drawn from the atomic, ionic and ionic-wave 'hydrogen' categories (DO_{192}, RE_{96} and MI_{48}) just as the physical body has its substrate materiality drawn from the macromolecular, micromolecular and atomic 'hydrogen' categories (DO_{768}, RE_{384} and MI_{192}). The active growth and maintenance forms and energies of the feeling (Kesdjan) body (FA_{24}) are of the H_{24} category, analogous to the active growth and maintenance forms and energies of the physical body (FA_{96}).

In the physical body, the growth and maintenance (or organic equilibrium) functions are referred to as homeostatic mechanisms.[24] We could refer to the note FA, in each evolutionary octave, as that level where balanced relationships between the "active elements"[25] within the particular body (physical, Kesdjan or Higher Being-body) are established and maintained.

Applying this principle to the emergent Kesdjan Body, homeostasis (or a balanced relationship between the active elements) will eventually be established at FA_{24}. The word "eventually" is critical to note here because, when man is considered in his typical half-awake, second-consciousness state, his feeling (emotional) world is neither balanced nor harmonious. It is, rather, an unbalanced mix of mechanical, negative and egoistic self-feelings that are manifestations of the crystallized consequences of the properties of the organ Kundabuffer. Instead of the maintenance energies and forms (active elements) which *nourish* the emotional life and the emergent Kesdjan Body in a harmonious way, there is a mish-mash of conflicting states that, at best, form a kind of vaporous, rapidly changing cloud in the feeling world.

The substrate materiality of Higher Being-body is drawn from the DO_{48}, RE_{24} and MI_{12} of the impressions octave (resulting from the first *conscious* shock). The material/vibrations of FA_6 in this octave (following on the second *conscious* shock) comprise the growth and maintenance active elements of Higher Being-body and are analogous to the FA_{24} and FA_{96} of the air and physical food octaves. We have posited that H_6 material/vibrations are intimately related to what Gurdjieff spoke of as *real* I or the Will (which appears *after* the $MI_{12} - FA_6$ interval of the second *conscious* shock).

Further notes in this octave concern the higher degrees of Reason (Degindad, Ternoonald, Podkoolad and Anklad).[26]

Analogies in the Digestive/Transformative Process of Physical Food, Air and Impressions

Digestion/transformation has two phases. The first is the process of 'taking apart' or *unbonding* the raw 'food' down to its elementals. The second phase (beginning at the FA of each octave) is the bonding of the elementals into new forms and/or energies that are compatible (or resonant) with the body it is intended to serve.

The first phase (the unbonding) takes place outside of the body it is to serve. This is a critical point to keep in mind. The lining cells of the gastrointestinal tract are like the skin in that they both mark the boundary or interface between what is outside the body and what is inside. In the instance of physical food, the *outside* is the interior of the gastrointestinal tract (mouth–stomach–intestine), which is a tube that extends from the mouth to the anus

---

24 Homeostasis – "The tendency of an organism to maintain a uniform and beneficial physiological stability within and between its parts." *Dorland's Illustrated Medical Dictionary*. In effect, it is a harmonious relationship between the forms and energies that comprise the respective bodies.
25 Gurdjieff, *Beelzebub's Tales*, p 761.
26 Ibid., pp 1176-77.

but whose *contents* lie *outside* of the physical body. This will be analogously true of the air and impressions octaves, namely, that during the taking-apart phase down to its elementals, the prospective food will lie outside the body it is intended to serve (Kesdjan Body in the case of air and Higher Being-body in the case of impressions).

Also to keep in mind is the marked contrast between the milieu of the stomach (highly acidic) and that of the small intestine (highly alkaline). The different environments allow for an acceleration of certain unbondings that are critical to full digestion. A parallel difference occurs in the milieux provided by the RE and MI of the air and impressions octaves.

Physical food *enters* the body during its passage from MI to FA (across the mechano-coinciding-Mdnel-In[27] or MI–FA interval). During this step, the elementals of physical food (amino acids, simple sugars and fats) are absorbed across the gastrointestinal membrane into the blood and lymph vessels. This MI–FA process occurs at the same time as oxygen of the air is absorbed into the body across the lung membrane. It is important to emphasize that the oxygen of air lies outside of the body during its passage down the bronchial tubes to the microscopic air sacs (alveoli). It is only when the oxygen passes across this inner cell membrane into the bloodstream that we can properly say that it has entered the body. Examination of the inner circulation of the enneagram (in particular the counter-movement from point 4 (FA_{96}) to point 2 (MI_{192}) will reveal an important relationship between the absorption of air and the absorption of the physical food elementals. An analogous process takes place in regard to the MI–FA intervals of the air and impressions octaves.

Passage from FA_{96} to SOL_{48} of physical food is the transition from mass-based material/vibrations to non-mass-based electromagnetic waveforms and fields. An analogous change in energy forms will take place at the massless FA–SOL intervals in both the air and the impressions octaves.

At FA_{96} the elementals of these food substances have been transformed into "active elements"[28] that carry out the majority of the maintenance functions of the physical body. Analogously, the note FA of both the air and impressions octaves will represent the energy level of the maintenance functions of Kesdjan Body and Higher Being-body.

The note SOL (point 5 in all evolutional octaves) marks the entry into the Harnel-Aoot,[29] the 'disharmonized' fifth Stopinder. In the instance of physical food, the SOL_{48} of neural impulses marks the entry into this Stopinder. DO_{48} of impressions (point 6) carries impulses from all *other* (the outside world of all other life-forms and things) and is the 'food' of potential relationships; the establishment of the individual person within the matrix of the Universe.

There is a high degree of hazard in the passage through the Harnel-Aoot, as the form of relationship between the individual and the rest of the Universe is to be determined by what takes place here. In the case of the physical body,

---

27 Gurdjieff, *Beelzebub's Tales*, P 754.
28 Ibid., P 759.
29 See glossary.

the influences of the instinctive-moving center (patterns established by DNA and other aspects of Itoklanoz) are predominant. If no *conscious* shock enters at point 6 (between SOL and LA), the type of physical relationship, which demonstrates itself at point 7 (LA), is *automatically* determined. For example, if one's upbringing has emphasized that you must always respect and unquestioningly follow the directives of one's elders and a situation arises where an older person emphatically directs you to "get them another martini," you will do so without question—without pausing to establish your presence or to evaluate the wisdom of their directive. In addition, there would be little or no sounding of FA_{24} of the air octave or of RE_{24} of the impressions octave. An analogous hazard will be present at the disharmonized fifth Stopinder of the air and impressions octaves.

Ordered patterns or formal relationships appear at the note LA in evolutional octaves. This often represents a step in the process of bonding into new resonant forms. In the case of the octave of physical food, the note LA represents the organizing power (in electromagnetic field *patterns* held within the molecular forms of the DNA and RNA unique to the life-form) and the end point in the organization of neural waveform impulses (SOL_{48}) into the *images* deriving from the five external senses. The note LA (in all three octaves) is, then, a sounding of the fundamental organizing principles[30] of the body (whether that "body" is the planetary, Kesdjan or Higher Being).

In all evolutional octaves, the note SI represents both the imminent completion of the octave and the generative possibilities inferred by its continuance. It simultaneously manifests a level of freedom from the efforts involved in reaching the LA and is the source of creative active elements which point to the future.

In a number of intervals, (e.g., DO–RE, RE–MI, FA–SOL, and LA–SI), Gurdjieff points to the principle or law of Harnel-miaznel[31] which, in the present case, refers to a 'higher' force, already present within the body, acting on a 'lower' force (a more dense 'hydrogen') to produce a 'middle' (a 'hydrogen' between the 'higher' and 'lower'). When this principle is applied to the digestion of physical food, it refers to the presence of active substances (enzymes, ions) and, later, electromagnetic fields and energies produced by the body, which act as the 'higher' in various stages of the digestive process. In order for these active substances to be formed, the body must expend energy almost all of which is lost by elimination in some form. In analogous fashion, the principle of Harnel-miatznel, at the same intervals, applies to the octaves of air and impressions.

Work on oneself requires effort and a large portion of the energy involved in this effort will be lost. However, the energy *gained* from the food greatly exceeds the loss.

---

30 Here we are concerned with an evolutional octave, whereas the organizing principles initially enter during the passage through the involutional octave of Creation (DO–SI–LA, etc.).
31 Rendered in *The Tales* in two different spellings, pp 751 and 786.

THE POTENCY OF POINT 6

On the enneagram of the digestion of the three foods, point 6 occupies an extraordinarily potent position.

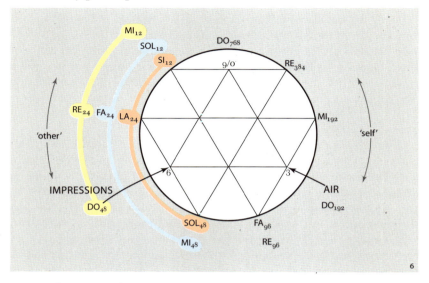

It is the point of incoming impressions, representing the interface or juncture between the 'self' and 'other'. How self (the individual) meets other (the outer world) – in assigning meanings, exploring, coming to relationships, giving significance to and in manifesting – is set in motion at this point. As previously mentioned, how this note (DO_{48}) is approached, is intimately related to the alternative and hazardous resolutions of the Harnel-Aoot of the physical food octave.

It is the point where Gurdjieff places the first *conscious* shock (the effort to self-remember). The shock brings energy to the sounding of DO_{48}. It represents the potential entry point into the third state of consciousness (what he also called the "consciousness of one's being").[32] The entry into the third state of consciousness is also the point at which a 'presence' ~ an inner separated *witness* ~ first enters.

With the first *conscious* shock, sufficient energy is given to the MI_{48} of the air octave to assist it across its MI–FA interval to FA_{24}. This shock also provides sufficient energy to initiate the progression of the impressions octave to RE_{24} and MI_{12}. What is not referred to directly, but which is experientially confirmed, is that efforts to self-remember also influence the processes taking place in the passage of SOL_{48} to LA_{24} of the physical food octave. Images of the external world emerging at LA_{24} are sharper, more intense and carry a 'weight' that is lacking in the half-sleep state. The *beingness* of what is imaged is more evident.

---

32 Ouspensky, *In Search*, p 141.

If no effort to self-remember is made, then all life processes (neural, biochemical and cellular) proceed "automatically."[33] In this circumstance, real choice is not possible, in spite of our half-sleep conviction that choices are made. The determinants of our thinking, feeling and moving are wholly circumscribed by the past, (by our Itoklanoz).

The effort to self-remember introduces the actual possibility of choice. Initiating the existence of a 'presence' that is separated from the processes of moving, feeling and thinking offers the opportunity to begin to escape from the prison of mechanicalness ~ in other words, to enter a world where choices can be *real*.

Lower and Higher Hydrogens

While each 'food' has a majority of its constituents drawn from one hydrogen category (H_{768} for physical food, H_{192} for air, H_{48} for impressions), this does not mean that other 'hydrogens' are not actually or potentially present in any given food. As Gurdjieff notes, with respect to air:

> "Let us suppose that the air we breathe is composed of twenty different elements unknown to our science. A certain number of these elements are absorbed by every man when he breathes. Let us suppose that five of these elements are always absorbed. Consequently the air exhaled by every man is composed of fifteen elements; five of them have gone to feeding the organism. But some people exhale not fifteen but only ten elements, that is to say, they absorb five elements more. These five elements are higher 'hydrogens.' These higher 'hydrogens' are present in every small particle of air we inhale. By inhaling air we introduce these higher 'hydrogens' into ourselves, but if our organism does not know how to extract them out of the particles of air, and retain them, they are exhaled back into the air."[34]

Higher Hydrogens

What could the "higher 'hydrogens'" be that are referred to in the above quotation? The higher 'hydrogens' (relative to air, H_{192}) would begin at RE_{96} and extend further to include 'hydrogens' 48, 24, 12 and 6 ("matters of our psychic and spiritual life on different levels."[35] In the chapter "Gurdjieff's 'hydrogens'" in *Perspectives*, we posit that, with H_{48} the worlds of mass-based categories of materiality are left behind and the worlds of neural impulses, images/impressions and the power of attention are entered. This view would infer that the higher hydrogens that he refers to would be of the nature of emotional values, intellectual images and impressions reinforced by directed attention.

33 Gurdjieff, *Beelzebub's Tales*, p 756.
34 Ouspensky, *In Search*, p 189.
35 Ibid., p 175.

With respect to physical food, there are substances that are indigestible by a human's stomach and intestines and have to be eliminated, (e.g., 'wood' or H_{1572} – includes substances like cellulose and lignin which can be food for certain animals but not for man; 'iron' or H_{3072} – includes minerals that, in small quantities, are essential to man's health, whereas in large quantities they are toxic). The trace minerals do undergo a degree of digestion, as they must be brought to the ionic (charged) state in order to function in the body. Physical food may also contain higher 'hydrogens' (for example, the images of H_{24} level) that reflect the manner in which it is prepared, the motivation of the cook and the aesthetic qualities of its presentation. These features provide sensory, emotional and intellectual impressions (H_{48}, H_{24} and higher) all of which are 'food' for each brain.

THE FIRST *CONSCIOUS* SHOCK

> "'… not one of you has noticed… that *you do not remember yourselves*.' (He gave particular emphasis to these words.) 'You do not feel *yourselves*; you are not conscious of *yourselves*. With you, "it observes" just as "it speaks," "it thinks," "it laughs." You do not feel: *I* observe, *I* notice, *I* see. Everything still "is noticed," "is seen." … In order really to observe oneself one must first of all *remember oneself*.' (He again emphasized these words.) 'Try to *remember yourselves* when you observe yourselves and later on tell me the results. Only those results will have any value that are accompanied by self-remembering. Otherwise you yourselves do not exist in your observations.'"[36]

Without the effort to self-remember, work-on-oneself devolves into imagination, 'thinking about' and 'feeling about', with no possibility of self-transformation existing because one inevitably remains in the second state of consciousness. Henri Tracol emphatically summarizes this point:

> "If we have chosen this theme above all others to elaborate upon, it is because the Practice of Remembering Oneself is the master key to Gurdjieff's teaching. It is the Alpha and Omega, the threshold that must be passed at the outset and crossed and recrossed time and again. It is also the musical 'silent pause' of complete realization, since any man capable of reaching it would know in their entirety the inner and outer relationships of his own being. He would be completely himself and able eventually to take his true place in the Universe.
>
> It must also be said that remembering oneself admits of an infinite number of approaches. It can be looked at from many and varied angles, it has certain definite degrees and stages and there is always more in it than we can ever grasp."[37]

---

36 Ouspensky, *In Search*, PP 117-18.
37 Henri Tracol, *George Ivanovitch Gurdjieff: Man's Awakening and the Practice of Remembering Oneself* (London: Pembridge Design Studio Press, 1987), P 12.

This premier *conscious* effort is placed at the point of the incoming impressions, at point 6, the entrance of DO_{48} on the enneagram of the three foods, (see prior illustration 3).

Before considering the continuance of the impressions and air octaves (to RE_{24} and FA_{24}, and MI_{12} and SOL_{12}), we will present a perspective on the first *conscious* shock that focuses on the initial stages of one's work on *Being*. Gurdjieff's statement, "You do not feel *yourselves*; you are not conscious of *yourselves*" applies to the precise moment during which the impression is being registered. There is also the clear implication that the aim is for this to become a persisting and, eventually, more persistent, willed *state* rather than a transient or momentary event.

Work on *Being*

It is also our understanding that efforts to establish the state of self-remembering are intimately related to the triadic nature of *Being*; namely the aspects which concern thinking (intellectual *being*), feeling (emotional *being*) and sensory-motor (physical *being*). One conclusion drawn from this perspective is that a person can truly say "I AM," only when he or she is, simultaneously, present in all three centers. This is not an easily established state, but one that requires persistent efforts that, for long periods of time, are partial or incomplete. For example, to be 'present to' (aware of) but 'separate from' (non-identified with) thinking is a considerable accomplishment; to be *present* to but separate from both thinking and feeling is far more difficult; to be 'present to' but 'separate from' thinking, feeling and sensory/motor *simultaneously* is a quite rare accomplishment, established only after commensurate efforts.

The first *conscious* shock (the effort to self-remember) refers to *all* efforts, however partial they may be, that aim to establish a *presence* or a *witness* within any or all of the three aspects of our *being*.

With each effort to self-remember, there may be an extremely brief interval in which there is a presence, *without* reference to what that presence is present *to*. Immediately following this, one becomes aware of the process of thinking or feeling or sensation-motion that is taking place in the present moment. One then has the opportunity to *direct* the attention.

Gurdjieff provided a host of exercises and tasks that focus the effort of self-remembering on one or more of the three aspects of *being*. Tasks such as the efforts to be present to the first mouthful of food, whenever one flushes the toilet or when one crosses the threshold of a door are examples of an effort focused on a specific event. The three-finger exercise described in *Life is Real*[38] and the variety of sensing exercises that, at later stages, are added to certain Movements and Sacred Dances, are characteristic of other, more complex efforts. Among the most fundamental is that which concerns 'following the breath'. He provided a clear description of this effort in *Life is Real*.

---

38 Gurdjieff, *Life is real only then, when "I am,"* PP 113-15.

Directed Attention and the Breath[39]

In the ordinary, half-sleep state of man (the second state of consciousness), the portions of air that can be food for the emotional and intellectual functions are either not taken in at all or are taken in to a much reduced degree. The degree to which those substances are to be taken in or absorbed is relative to the degree of the individual's capacity for directed attention.[40]

To approach the emotional and intellectual components of the food of air requires consideration of a person's *subjective* experience, because *directed attention* is required for those substances to be taken in or absorbed. Verification of this assertion, in terms of measurable physiological changes that result, can be inferred but has not been experimentally confirmed at the present time.[41] It is also difficult to select specific descriptive terms for these substances because of the subjective nature of individual experiences. Also, if a person has not made the necessary effort of directed attention, he or she has no individual experience to use as a comparator. In this case, he or she will likely conclude that the results reported by others are the products of intellectual theorizing or imagination.

In illustration 7, note that the points 9/0, 3 and 6 lie *inside* the outer circle (the flow of the event). The inner placement implies that energies must enter from inside (at the outer apices of the three *being* triads in blue) for the three octaves to be initiated and completed. In the case of physical food, there must be a 'thrust' from within some aspect of the third brain which will motivate the body toward placing food in the mouth.[42]

In the case of air, the instinctive center initiates and sustains the cyclicity of breathing in order to preserve life. In the case of impressions, there is a passive registration but no active initiation. This passive registration is not sufficient to energize either the air octave beyond MI_{48} or the impressions octave at DO_{48} beyond its own weak sounding. The images that appear at LA_{24} of the food octave (derived from the five senses of the first brain) are passively accepted as being unqualifiedly real and an automatic reaction is foreordained.

When the first *conscious* shock is applied (via efforts to self-remember) point 6 is energized from *inside*. In this effort, a portion of the power of the attention (H_{12}) is brought to the entry of incoming impressions (via the inner circulatory line 8 to 5). A presence appears that is not the impression itself or any part of the process that leads to the resultant images (H_{24} at point 7). Because it is evanescent at best, we cannot call this presence a permanent and singular I, but we clearly recognize a distinct sense of a 'self' (a nascent I?)

---

39 Buzzell, *Perspectives*, chapter 9, "Gurdjieff's 'hydrogens'," p 129.
40 Buzzell, *Explorations*, chapter 7, pp 106-7 and chapter 12, pp 276-77.
41 Such verification may well be forthcoming, particularly via measurable increases in H_{96} substances and in increased neural activity within the brain. The interactions taking place between the Dalai Lama and the neuroscience community is an example of this effort, as reported in the Mind and Life Conferences.
42 See commentary on the frog experiments on p 113 in this chapter.

that can be and *is* present to, but separated from, the evolving impression. Over time, and with many repeated efforts, this presence can grow in strength, duration and clarity.

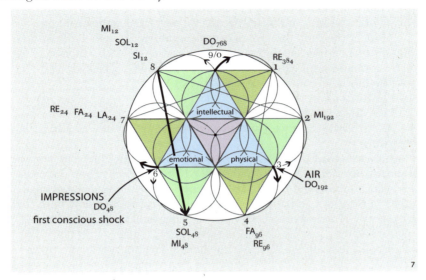

Direct Perceptions

Efforts to be present to the breath are a critical aspect of becoming more conscious of our emotional (feeling) *being* and physical (moving-motor) *being*. The heavy arrow drawn on the symbol (figure 8) illustrates this point.

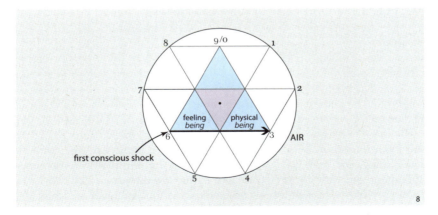

We understand the higher 'hydrogens' of the air to be the results of "direct perceptions," because they do not require 'thinking about' or reasoning (neural processes that are further on in the digestive octave). They are immediately obvious; they are facts that result from the application of directed attention to the act of breathing.[43] The direct perceptions listed below result from directed attention being held on the breath during quiet sitting as well as during ordinary daily activities.

~ Breathing is a recurring, cyclic event. There is a slight effort at the initiation of inspiration and a 'letting go' at the start of expiration.

~ Most of the time, breathing is a pleasant experience – a filling up and a release. Depending on daily events, in particular with emotional states and physical activity, it can be rapid, forced, shallow or briefly interrupted.

~ There is no choice in breathing – I *must* breathe.

~ The air is always there – it surrounds me.

~ I am alive, in part, because I breathe.

~ As I breathe, I notice that other living beings breathe. I share the act of breathing.

~ I am aware of a 'something' (an expanding, soft, vibratory sensation) that during expiration, moves out into all parts of the body from the chest.

~ As one follows the breath, an awareness of the movement and changing tensions in the chest and abdomen, enter the consciousness and, with that, a linkage between sensing the body and following the breath is established.

This perception is in sharp contrast to that which is produced by my usual, second state of consciousness, (where I have no continuous awareness of my body or of my breath). This can be a recurrent and startling perception; one that carries an intimation of how profoundly different the third state of consciousness is. This brief description represents a mere 'crack-in-the-door' into the vast and varied worlds of feeling and sensation. In actuality, it is the sounding of a stronger and deeper DO of air and the imparting of greater energy to the MI – FA interval of food. Further steps in these two octaves are enlivened by this effort. Many increasingly subtle direct perceptions arise when this practice becomes well-established. They could be understood as representing some of the higher 'hydrogens' of air which are referred to in *In Search*.[44]

The Body

The sensing of parts, or the whole, of the planetary body is the effort to establish a 'presence' or a 'witness', within the body. In a state of sensing, there is a clear inner separation between the emergent I and the awareness of the *being* of the planetary body. Because we are given, in the second state of consciousness, a degree of automatic awareness of our body, we may not initially appreciate how profound and subtle are the direct perceptions that result from *intentionally* sensing parts or all of the body. Gurdjieff provided a host of tasks and exercises, in many sequences and for many circumstances, that demand our best effort to train and divide the attention. The overall aim is to initiate and establish a presence which is simultaneously aware of itself and aware of the *beingness* of the planetary body.

---

43 In these descriptions, we have tried to separate direct perceptions from the rapid thought process that lawfully follows on the perception. Because of the rapid velocity of the inner circulation, it is difficult to be aware of this separation.

44 Ouspensky, *In Search*, P 184.

Prolonged and determined practices of following the breath and sensing the body lead to ever deeper and more subtle direct perceptions. These are efforts that are intimately related to the transformation (digestion) of the sensate and feeling functions which open into the world of *being*.

The Mind

Gurdjieff also provided many approaches through which the reality and fundamental purpose of our intellectual (thinking) *being* begins to be revealed. The aim of the following two *being* tasks are illustrative of this effort: to be present with the first mouthful of food and to remember yourself as you cross a threshold (whether it is a physical, emotional or thinking threshold), illustration 9.

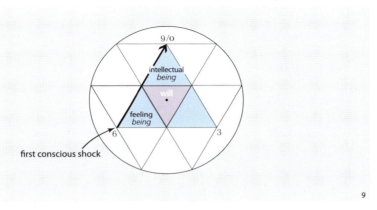

9

With these tasks, an effort to enliven point 9/0 (the apex of intellectual *being*) is the aim. In ordinary life (the second state of consciousness) one is unaware that each and every action taken (however small/large it may be) requires an activating impulse, originating from within our intellectual *being*, into the unfolding event. This is true even for one-brained (cold-blooded) beings, as is demonstrated when the outer coating of brain cells (the germinal third brain) is removed. The creatures (which were frogs in most of the experiments) initiate no action into the outside world–they sit passively and fall over dead after several days. If food is pushed into the mouth, they will swallow and digest the food. If they are pushed into water, they will swim, climb out of the water and sit. From within themselves, they cannot initiate any movement or engage the external world in any way.

From within a human's intellectual *being*, a commitment into action, an interaction with the world, must emerge. It is the carrier of the Holy-Affirming force into life. Among the many possibilities, the two tasks noted create the circumstances wherein a 'presence' can begin to appear at the very moment of commitment into an action by the whole of oneself. The nascent I, held separate from the *being* in that moment, can energize (*spiritualize*) the movement into the world.

Touching the Triadic Being

The effort to bring oneself into the state of self-remembering, coupled (via the divided attention) with following the breath, sensing and enlivening the commitment into life events, establishes an initial contact with each of the triads of one's *being*.

These efforts are only a beginning. The helpmates that Gurdjieff has provided include many other aspects of Work on *being* which incorporate the three brains, both alone and in various combinations, via the Movements and Sacred Dances, group work, the music, the study of his written Legominism and a multitude of individual tasks.

The effort to enter and inhabit the third state of consciousness is, however, the "threshold that must be passed at the outset and crossed and recrossed time and again."[45]

Our exploration presently concerns the first *conscious* shock but, inferentially, we can see that the second *conscious* shock will further *spiritualize* the *being* triads and help to complete the "consciousness of one's being"[46] (illustration 10).

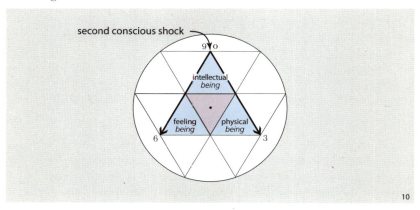

Work on Function: Enabling the Digestion of Air and Impressions

The prior segments focused on the critical and persevering efforts to establish the state of self-remembering and to initiate work on *being*. Our aim in this and subsequent segments is to explore possible ways to view the process of the further digestion or transformation/evolution of the octaves of air and impressions. These efforts are not separate from work on *being*, as all real Work influences every aspect of *function*, *being* and *will*. It is distinctive, however, because the powers of the third state of consciousness are brought to bear on the sensory, feeling and thinking impressions that derive from the functional aspects of the three brains.

---

45 Tracol, *Gurdjieff: Man's Awakening and the Practice of Remembering Oneself*, P 12.
46 Ouspensky, *In Search*, P 141.

Inner Separation

A consistent and separated 'presence' is essential for this transformational process. All efforts to self-observe become introspection (one center observing another center) if the state of self-remembering is not established. While useful information can be acquired by introspection, the process of transformation is not actualized.

The first, most essential 'seeing', which derives from self-remembering and the effort to self-observe, is a discovery about the nature of the images that appear at RE_{24}, FA_{24} and LA_{24}. In the second state of consciousness, the impressions deriving from our senses (LA_{24}) are mechanically taken as 'real'. In the third state of consciousness, the realization is made that all images are constructions of the brains. Our sensations, feelings and thoughts are 'seen' as functional images, automatically produced by the first, second and third brains. Their reality becomes instantly *conditioned* or *relative*. The full import of this observation takes considerable time to realize.

Digestion beyond 'hydrogen $_{96}$'

In *Perspectives*, chapter 9 (pages 115-49), we introduced the notion that the categories of mass-based materiality extended from H_{3072} ('iron'), to H_{1536} ('wood'), H_{768} ('food'), H_{384} ('water'), H_{192} ('air') and H_{96} (ionic matter). Beyond this, as Gurdjieff noted, "'Hydrogens' 48, 24, 12 and 6 are matters unknown to physics and chemistry, matters of our psychic and spiritual life on different levels."[47] We proposed to view H_{48} as *non*-mass-based ionic waveforms and H_{24} H_{12} and H_6 as categories of other electromagnetic phenomena (em fields, photons and the em force itself).

It was not until the latter part of the 1920s, with the first brainwave (electroencephalograph or EEG) studies, that the electromagnetic basis of neural and brain activity was made clear. Even though an enormous amount of research into nervous system functions has taken place since then, there remain unanswered questions regarding such fundamental issues as the nature of the images that are experienced by brained beings and the existential status of attention and states of consciousness.

Given that these issues are unresolved, we have posited that all neural impulses are of the category H_{48} (ionic waveforms) and that the images we perceive (whether physical, emotional or intellectual) are of the category H_{24}; the result of interaction between the ionic waveforms (H_{48} – the incoming and associative neural impulses) and the fluctuating and complex electromagnetic field produced by the cells of the brain.

From this perspective, we view consciousness as an attribute of *all* brained life, the breadth and depth of its states being determined by the evolutionary development of the brains and by the variable application of the attention (H_{12}).

---

47 Ouspensky, *In Search*, P 175. These words were spoken circa 1915.

We have posited the category H_{12} to be photonic energy (light waves) which functions as the carrier of the generative powers of attention. Attention (considered as the entire category of H_{12}) can function automatically (via the instinctive center functions and early learned behaviors) or be *independently directed* by the Will (H_6). In the language of physics, H_6 would be a manifestation of the electromagnetic force itself.

This perspective on the "psychic and spiritual" hydrogens makes it possible to ask, "If the higher 'hydrogens' are digestive products (represented by the FA_{24}–RE_{24}, and SOL_{12}–MI_{12} of the air and impressions octaves–with the first *conscious* shock applied), how can we understand them as having been contained in the 'elementalness' of air and impressions, in the same way that higher hydrogens are contained in physical food?"

Our line of reasoning begins with a consideration of physical food (H_{768}). Within the complex, macromolecular structure of any food (DO_{768}) lie the electromagnetic field patterns that have determined the mass-based form of the particular food. These electromagnetic field patterns (which are of the category H_{24}) are unknown and 'unseen' when we begin the digestive octave of physical food, but they are there and can be discovered if the 'digestive' process is carried to the level of H_{24} (the electromagnetic field patterns that are the final determinants of the structural form of the DNA). What has been 'discovered' (or 'digested to') are expressions or embodiments of law that determine the manifestations in *lower*, more dense worlds.

This principle is seen in the earlier steps in the octave of digestion. For example, the category of H_{96} (ions, both atomic and molecular) acts on macromolecular structures (H_{384}) to produce micromolecular and atomic forms (H_{192} – the digestive products we called the elementals of physical food – the amino acids, fatty acids and simple sugars). Similarly, the category H_{24} (electromagnetic fields) acts on ions (H_{96}) to produce the massless ionic waveforms (H_{48}) that function as nerve impulses.

Aspects of each higher category of a hydrogen have always been present (essentially hidden within forms of the lower hydrogen category) and are revealed when investigations are carried on up to that level.

To discover the higher hydrogen requires the application of attention (H_{12}) and the powers of reasoning (the application of attentioned awareness; the practice of self-remembering). The discovery obviously does not happen by itself. The *seeing* of successive embodiments of law (*principle*) is a metaphorical seeing (simile, allegory, analog or similitude).

THE INNER CIRCULATIONS

Each of the three foods contributes to the functioning of the physical (instinctive-moving), emotional (feeling) and intellectual (thinking) centers, even though their entry points into the body are different. Or, it could be said that each of the three foods contains forms and energies that are *potential* foods for each of the centers (brains). This point is made more clear when reference is made to the three-octave enneagram of food and the connections established by the inner circulation are considered.

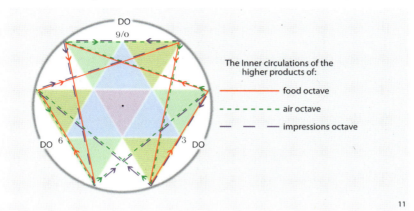

11

The overlay of the 1-4-2-8-5-7 of the inner circulations of all three octaves of 'food' is shown (illustration 11). Energetic influences flow between the three centers, via the inner circulation, potentially establishing a blending of the digestive products of the three foods. In *Perspectives* (chapter 11) and *Explorations* (chapter 12), more detailed discussions are undertaken which focus on how these influences are related to one's inner work and one's self-transformation.

A degree of relativity has to be appreciated with respect to the notion that each of the three foods provides potential nourishment for all three centers (and subcenters).[48] The proteins of physical food primarily contribute to the physical structure of the body (to the formation and replacement of tissues and organs), although the micromolecular structure of enzymes, transmitters, hormones and vitamins are also protein based. Sugars and fats are more closely related to the physical energy systems of the body (both for immediate use and for storage), although they also contribute to combinations of amino acids, fats and sugars in many essential intracellular processes – including vital aspects of the function of the brain as a whole.

As just previously noted in the case of the oxygen in air, the primary digestive use is in providing energies and forms for the physical body. However, there are hormones and neuropeptides (derived from the H_{96} digestive products of oxygen) that clearly influence the function of emotional and intellectual centers. Knowing this, we could ask, "What are the elemental food substances contained in air which are resonant with the needs of the emotional and intellectual centers?"

At first glance, impressions appear more clearly differentiated into sensory-motor, emotional (feeling) and intellectual (thinking) images. On

---

[48] Ouspensky discusses the subcenters in the Fifth Lecture, *The Psychology of Man's Possible Evolution* (New York: Vintage Books, 1974), pp 107-14.

closer examination, however, elements of the impressions that relate to the other centers can be found in all three. For example:

> ~ facial expressions and tones of voice are sensory images of the physical world that also contain great varieties of food (as meaning) for the emotional and intellectual centers;
>
> ~ words such as "hate" and "devotion" are abstract images formed in the intellectual center, but their emotional and physical meanings also serve to nourish these two centers;
>
> ~ a well-cooked meal, visually pleasing and aesthetically arranged, provides nourishment for the emotional and intellectual centers as well as being the primal food for the physical body.

In the following quotation, Gurdjieff discusses the interrelatedness of the three octaves of foods by using the principle of analogy (metaphor). This method of discourse makes it possible, as we noted earlier, to discuss the three octaves that comprise Reality (Absolute–Sun; Sun–Earth; Earth–Moon) in a resonant manner. We have added (in brackets) the expressions "Kesdjan Body" and "Higher Being-body" to the expressions "astral" and "mental."

> "Inner growth, the growth of the inner bodies of man, the astral [Kesdjan Body], the mental [Higher Being-body], and so on, is a material process completely analogous to the growth of the physical body. In order to grow, a child must have good food, his organism must be in a healthy condition to prepare from this food the material necessary for the growth of the tissues. The same thing is necessary for the growth of the 'astral body'; out of the various kinds of food entering it, the organism must produce the substances necessary for the growth of the 'astral body.' Moreover, the 'astral body' requires for its growth the same substances as those necessary to maintain the physical body, only in much greater quantities. If the physical organism begins to produce a sufficient quantity of these fine substances and the 'astral body' within it becomes formed, this astral organism will require for its maintenance less of these substances that it required during its growth. The surplus from these substances can then be used for the formation and growth of the 'mental body' which will grow with the help of the same substances that feed the 'astral body,' but of course the growth of the 'mental body' will require more of these substances than the growth and feeding of the 'astral body.'"[49]

Entry into the Impressions Octave — the Triad RE_{24}–FA_{24}–LA_{24}

With the first *conscious* shock, the impressions octave proceeds to RE_{24}, the air octave is assisted across its MI_{48}–FA_{24} interval and SOL_{48} of the food octave is enhanced in its passage to LA_{24}. The triad RE_{24}–FA_{24}–LA_{24} is sounded.

---

49 Ouspensky, *In Search*, p 180.

Human Transformation

Images are formed from the material/vibrations of H_{24} (electromagnetic waveforms interacting with em fields). LA_{24} includes all of the images deriving from the external senses of the first brain (the outer world). FA_{24} includes all the images deriving from the inner senses of the second brain (the inner, feeling world). RE_{24} includes all the images deriving from the abstracting functions performed by the third brain, (e.g., language, number, the concept of laws). As a result of the first *conscious* shock, a 'presence' or witness appears which can be selectively 'aware of', yet inwardly 'separated from', the images produced by the three brains.[50] We chose the word "selectively" because the images created are at different notes in their respective octaves:

RE_{24}–abstracting/thinking; FA_{24}–feeling; LA_{24}–sensation/motion;

△ At the note RE, all evolutional octaves have barely begun; not even the long-term aims having been defined. Its potential, then, is both very large and poorly defined. In addition, the MI–FA interval and the disharmonized fifth Stopinder have not as yet been encountered.

△ At the note FA, the fundamental internal structure and maintenance energies of the body to be served have appeared, in part because the aims have been defined at the sounding of MI and also from interaction with that which enters from 'outside' (at its mechano-coinciding-Mdnel-In). However, the progression of the evolutional octave has still not yet encountered the fifth Stopinder (which will define its inner relationship to the 'outer' Universe).

△ At the note LA, the category of material/vibrations determines the form or pattern of that which is the aim of the entire evolutional octave.

△ The possible futures that lie within the material/vibrations of the note SI include the capacity to encapsulate (incorporate/blend as *one*) the essence of each of the prior steps. This essence has the potential, then, to initiate an entirely new octave.

Each note of evolutional octaves shares the resonant characteristics noted above. Therefore, the results of being 'present' to the triad of RE_{24}–FA_{24}–LA_{24} are extremely subtle and complex. *The effort to maintain the separation of a presence from the created images is the key* to the potency inherent in self-remembering. If one loses this state of separation, *identification* with the image instantly takes place; in a sense, the 'I' becomes or disappears into the image (it is forgotten).

If one is able to maintain inner separation and presence, then a number of perceptions (evidence of higher 'hydrogens') appear. The most essential perception resulting from the direct 'seeing' is that the images (the impressions at RE_{24}–FA_{24}–LA_{24}) are products of the brain's functioning. The bodies and motions in the external world, the feelings of the inner world and the words, ideas, formulations and other constructions of the abstract (thinking) world

---

50 While it is useful to speak of the RE–FA–LA images as if they were separate, a three-brained being most frequently experiences them as one, coalesced image (an image having thinking, feeling and sensory-motor aspects). Attentive observation reveals this triadic nature.

are seen to have only a relative reality. All of them are deeply dependent on the past (the prior functional expressions of the brains), which includes all of the influences that flow from Itoklanoz.[51]

Within this 'seeing' lies a great freedom—emerging from the clear recognition that I (whatever that 'presence' is) am *not* the images. What is seen is the "automatic" flow of three-brained images that are lawful results of the biology and biochemistry of the planetary body. Work on *being*, which should go on simultaneously, strengthens the presence and, in a sense, rescues and enables the witness or embryonic I by forging an increasingly real domain of AMNESS with which it can meld.

The Fourth Way

At this point, it is important to underscore a fundamental difference between the Fourth Way and other spiritual paths; that which Gurdjieff referred to as the paths of man number 1 (with the center-of-gravity focused in the body), man number 2 (with the center-of-gravity in the feelings) and man number 3 (with the center-of-gravity in the mind). The Fourth Way brings together aspects of these three paths and enlivens the simultaneous work on all three centers with the continuing efforts to establish the third state of consciousness (self-remembering).

The Fourth way is also distinguished by its being conducted in the midst of ordinary life, whereas the other paths require varying degrees of isolation from family and community events and commitments. One could refer to Fourth Way work as simultaneous work on *function, being* and *will*, with the center-of-gravity of *function* in the planetary body and its "automatic" processes, the center-of-gravity of *being* in the emotional (feeling) center and the center-of-gravity of *will* in the thinking center.

To this metaphorical view needs to be added the qualification that *everything is related to everything else* and there are, thus, no arbitrary divisions between centers or between aspects of Work. Underlying all perspectives of what constitutes the Fourth Way, however, is Henri Tracol's emphasis on the "Alpha and Omega" of Gurdjieff's teaching: the continual efforts to remember the self.

Physical Food Octave — LA24

With this emphasis in mind, we return to the consideration of the images (H_{24}) of the three brains and the separated 'presence'. Reference was previously made to the differences between the notes RE, FA, and LA of any evolutional octave and to the fact that these differences infer three separate phases of octavic development. Specifically, first-brain images (LA_{24}) emerge close to the end of the physical food octave. They are, in a sense, 'complete' in their ordering or internal organized form or pattern. Their future does not lie in a change of form (or transformation). In other words, the images of the

---

51 Buzzell, *Explorations*, chapter 5, "The Duration of Being-existence," pp 67-83.

outside world (in vision, hearing, smell, taste and touch) remain what they are. What does change, via the power of attention implicit in self-remembering, is that inner details and previously hidden relationships become evident and this penetration into the interstices of the images greatly increases the amount of real data available to the associative processes of all three brains.

When this effort is fused with the *being*-effort of sensing the body (in whole or part), the breadth, depth and intensity of awareness of all sensation-motion is greatly increased. One becomes, simultaneously, more present to one's physical being *and* more aware of the body's functional capacities in both sensation and motion. Combining these efforts with work on the Sacred Dances and Movements introduces *attentioned motion*, which requires the reconciled participation of all three brains.

The body, as a directed and sensed instrument, becomes gradually infused with emotional values and reasoned understandings.

Air Octave — FA24

The circumstance with regard to FA$_{24}$ (feeling or emotional images) is quite different. The relational, or feeling, world has been deeply influenced by events taking place during the individual's Itoklanoz. In living this multitude of events (full of imitation, reinforcement and the crystallized consequences of the properties of the organ Kundabuffer), a plethora of mechanical reactions, negative states and egoistic impulses have been thoroughly implanted. They are, for the most part, accepted as real by the second state of consciousness and, unless self-remembering in some form occurs, one will live out their life directed by these automatic, externally imposed criteria for all relationships.

The entirety of one's life of relationships is exposed, over time, in the feeling images that one becomes aware of from the efforts to self-remember and self-observe. One of the first observations concerns all that we have *not* seen when in the second conscious state. This includes the predominantly passive and supportive role played by the thinking-center in many feeling states. Justifications and wordy denouncements are evidences of 'a-thinking;' the automatic processes of the thinking-center that are promulgated to support the negative or mechanical feeling. One becomes aware of the fact that this mechanical 'a-thinking' process accompanies, or follows on, almost all negative or mechanical states and rarely, if ever, is there evidence of an evaluative, inquiring thought process that is specifically and independently aware of the feeling itself. One also observes that the body is a participant in the kaleidoscope of feeling states, reflecting these states in muscle tensions, habitual postures, gestures, resonant facial expressions and tones of voice.

In order to observe the various types of entanglements of the three brains (or, said differently, to take three-brained 'pictures' of oneself), requires long and repeated efforts. At this stage, the effort to properly self-observe is not aimed at permanently changing or transforming the manifestation of the feeling state. They are aimed at *learning* about oneself, about how the three brains have come to be such intertwined and reactive instruments of automaticity. Gurdjieff emphasized this in his admonition to, "Try not to express negativity." "Try" is the key word here because, with this effort, the trying, we *see* more deeply into the complexity of the three brains; we see other associative connections, other 'causes' that lie deeper in the past. By trying to obstruct the manifestation, we see more deeply into that state. He did not expect us to be successful in our 'trying' (for a long time, negative feelings have a way of sneaking out, sooner or later anyway), but instead, offered a method that helps in observing more deeply into oneself.

Over time (often *much* time), certain mechanical and negative feeling states become less powerful—in both strength and duration. One way of viewing this change is to see the entire process as requiring a certain force of attention. As more of the force of attention goes into maintaining the *presence* and the impartial observation, there is *less* attention given to, or available to, the feeling state (and its accompanying 'a-thinking' and bodily reactions).

In addition, there are many methods that were given by Gurdjieff to assist in this process. For example, relaxing a bodily part that is usually tense during a particular emotional (feeling) state weakens the triadic relationship which is being maintained by the three centers (or subcenters). Sensing a part of the body introduces a conscious element into what had previously been a mechanical, "subconscious"[52] process. The same is true of following the breath or of many of the tasks and exercises that are a part of Fourth Way work.

In this segment, we have been focusing on the note FA_{24} (images) of the air (feeling) octave. At this note, the primary concern is learning more and more about one's inner world of feeling, observing it more broadly and deeply and strengthening the *presence* and the power of the directed attention. Simultaneous with this, as noted earlier, are the various efforts to establish an increasing presence within the three aspects of *being* (physical, emotional and intellectual).

Both of these efforts (described as work on *function* and work on *being*) proceed in tandem throughout one's life. What has been mentioned concerning FA_{24}, is only an introduction. A great deal more is contained in this 'hydrogen' category, including aspects of Work that concern relationship with other people in Work, as well as with all others. Additionally, the sacred impulse of Conscience plays an increasing role in the $FA_{24}-SOL_{12}$ process and, with that, directed attention and the enablement of the sacred impulses of Faith, Hope and Love can enter more surely into all aspects of 'feeling.'

From all of these efforts comes a strengthening of the resolve to Work. The confirmation of the reality of the three worlds (physical, feeling and thinking) which we can inhabit becomes the foundation of one's wish TO BE. The transformation of negative and mechanical emotions (feelings), however, has not yet taken place.

---

52 See *Beelzebub's Tales*, pp 24-26. Gurdjieff's view of the subconscious is different, in important respects, from the Freudian–Jungian conception.

Impressions (Thinking) Octave—RE$_{24}$

With the effort to self-remember and self-observe, thinking images (RE$_{24}$) that one becomes present to and aware of are initially comprised of the plethora of 'a-thinkings' that reflect the automatic associative processes of this form of mentation. The process is most often conducted using words, (e.g., 'talking to oneself'), although visual images, numbers, geometrical and other symbolic forms may be associatively utilized. There is considerable difference between individuals in the content of this 'a-thinking', reflecting wide variation in facility, training, education and subcenter function. One frequent feature is its justifying and supportive *passivity* (namely, that it is most often used by more assertive or affirming feelings (second brain) and/or sensation/motions (first brain). For example, one very often talks to oneself in justification or explanation of a particular feeling (such as anger) or sensation (such as hunger), but is not aware (with a separated *presence*) that this 'a-talking' is taking place. With continuing observation one notices that it is rather rare when one is *not* 'a-talking' about something or other. He also called this "perpetual chatter."[53] This automatic activity is semi-consciously recognized, even in the second state of consciousness, by such metaphorical terms as "wool-gathering," "mulling over," "thoughts being elsewhere," "absent mindedness," or "being preoccupied."

One also becomes aware of the dream-like quality of much of this subconscious activity, with a 'stream' of fantasy images which often include a replay of real events, subtly or not so subtly altered to defend, attack or justify one's emotional state. A surprising (and remorse-inducing) observation is that one automatically *lies* a good deal of the time. As Gurdjieff noted:

> "In the life of an ordinary man truth and falsehood have no moral value of any kind because a man can never keep to one single truth. His truth changes.... And a man can never *tell the truth*. Sometimes '*it tells*' *the truth*, sometimes '*it tells*' *a lie*."[54]

> "Speaking in general the most difficult barrier is the conquest of lying. A man lies so much and so constantly both to himself and to others that he ceases to notice it."[55]

To see and remain inwardly separated from the lying that takes place both "to himself and to others" is a severe challenge. The 'scald' produced by this recognition leads, appropriately, to remorse of conscience – but the struggle to remain inwardly 'separated' is still required. Over time, if one maintains the effort of inner separation, alternate possibilities begin to appear. For example, one sees more and more clearly that there is a deep, essence-leveled responsibility to stop lying and, on occasion, one is able to be silent in a circumstance where, previously, one had, in reaction to another person's statement, lied about what one had or had not done. In this event, a

---

53 Ouspensky, *In Search*, P 179.
54 Ibid., P 159.
55 Ibid., P 229.

change in one's inner attitude toward particular manifestations has become strong enough to allow for the possibility of a choice to be made (to remain silent). One sees the lie but does not permit its manifestation. Work on oneself proceeds in just such small steps. The power of directed attention, which makes possible proper self-observation, is further illustrated by these comments of Gurdjieff:

> "He begins to understand that self-observation is an instrument of self-change, a means of awakening. By observing himself he throws, as it were, a ray of light onto his inner processes which have hitherto worked in complete darkness. And under the influence of this light the processes themselves begin to change. There are a great many chemical processes that can take place only in the absence of light. Exactly in the same way many psychic processes can take place only in the dark. Even a feeble light of consciousness is enough to change completely the character of a process, while it makes many of them altogether impossible. Our inner psychic processes [our inner alchemy] ... have much in common with those chemical processes in which light changes the character of the process and they are subject to analogous laws."[56]

> "Identifying is the chief obstacle to self-remembering. A man who identifies with anything is unable to remember himself. In order to remember oneself it is necessary first of all *not to identify*. But in order to learn not to identify man must first of all *not be identified with himself*, must not call himself 'I' always and on all occasions. He must remember that there are two in him, that there is *himself*, that is 'I' in him, and there is *another* with whom he must struggle and whom he must conquer if he wishes at any time to attain anything."[57]

Thus, the initial aspects to be worked on, in the digestive octave of impressions, concern impartial observation, more and more deeply, into the images (RE_{24}, FA_{24}, LA_{24}) created by the brains. The struggle with identification is a never-ending one. Assisting this struggle are many exercises, exemplified by the thinking exercise (described in *Views from the Real World*)[58] and by the *Psychological Exercises and Essays* by A. R. Orage.[59] Working on these exercises initiates a process of disciplining the 'thinking apparatus' such that it can increasingly become a directed instrument of mentation.

The Triadic Theatre

Over time, one becomes increasingly aware of the three-aspectness of the automatically produced images. Regardless of whether thinking, feeling or sensation-motion predominate, the other two centers (and/or subcenters) are woven into resultant images. For example, one may find oneself, in the winter,

---

56 Ouspensky, *In Search*, P 146.
57 Ibid., P 151.
58 G.I. Gurdjieff, *Views from the Real World* (New York: Penguin Books, 1991), P 106.
59 A.R. Orage, *Psychological Exercises and Essays* (New York: Samuel Weiser, 1974).

shivering in below-zero temperatures. Automatically, words appear, "It is so cold," and, simultaneous there is a feeling that alters the way in which the words are spoken. Or, one is offended by what another person said and, along with this feeling, there are words spoken inwardly in an angry tone. Simultaneous with this reaction, is a clenching of the jaw and of a fist. On observing this kind of inner 'event' one has 'taken a picture' of three centers (and/or subcenters) blended into one flowing, automatic manifestation.

The recognition that the automatic inner-world 'theatre' is always triadic in construction (involving the participation of thinking, feeling and sensory-motor elements of the three centers/brains or their subcenters) is an important 'seeing' into the nature of one's automatic mentation processes. Also, the recognition of the triadic theatre has direct application to one's half-awake daily existence. What is underscored by these observations is that human beings are *always* three-brained. In many inner and outer world events, this is not immediately evident to the 'witness.' However, repeated efforts make clear that, to widely varying degrees, there is always a sensory-motor, feeling and thinking (abstraction) aspect to the flowing images of the inner world. It could be said that the human brain is so constructed that, at the level of 'hydrogen' $_{24}$, a triad of RE – FA – LA is always sounded.

In Sum
This consideration of the digestion of impressions is intended only as an introduction to the initial stages of the octave of the further digestion of food, air and impressions. Emphasis has been placed on the following features:

△ that DO_{48} represents the coalescence of the three octaves into an intimately related, or three-brained triadic progression;

△ that the effort to self-remember (to be *present* but to be separated from the activity of the brains) is the *sine qua non* of efforts toward self-transformation;

△ that a subtle, but powerful, *freedom* begins to appear which results from the establishment of a separated 'witness';

△ that with respect to RE_{24}–FA_{24}–LA_{24}, there are distinct attributes within the images which appear at the notes RE, FA and LA that are due to the different qualities of these notes in all evolutional octaves;

△ that self-observation (from the self-remembered state) is, for a long time, an educational process in which one sees more deeply and broadly into one's 'mechanical' or automatic past. A three-dimensional perspective is gained on the task of true self-transformation. The task becomes understood as a life-long enterprise;

△ that directed attention, when brought to bear on mentation processes that previously had taken place 'in the dark' of the subconscious, can alter or interrupt this mechanical process.

While changes in behavior begin to appear, true self-transformation lies further ahead.

The Creative Attention — MI_{12}–SOL_{12}–SI_{12}

In the triadic sounding of MI_{12}–SOL_{12}–SI_{12}, the three "changed"[60] intervals in an octave are being approached: the mechano-coinciding-Mdnel-In (MI–FA of impressions), the Harnel-Aoot (SOL–LA of air) and the intentionally-actualized-Mdnel-In (SI–DO of physical food). Each has potentials and hazards that mark their passage as the second *conscious* shock is approached.

From what Gurdjieff has said, it can be concluded that *real* I coalesces (within the emergent Higher Being-body) as the MI_{12}–FA_6 of impressions (the second *conscious* shock) is crossed and that the Kesdjan Body (with its growth and maintenance energies in place) has taken form. Neither body is 'complete' at this stage. FA_6 of Higher Being-body will move to complete its octave by the attainment of higher degrees of Reason. LA_6 of Kesdjan Body will move to the SI of its octave in the creative exploration/expression of compassion and service.

Beyond emphasizing certain fundamental qualities and attributes, we will say little about this triadic sounding. Gurdjieff did not speak in detail about it, preferring metaphorical approaches to this critical interval/stage in self-transformation. In *In Search*, he provides guidance regarding certain of the principles involved.

> "For the two octaves [air and impressions] to develop further, a second *conscious* shock is needed at a certain point in the machine, a new conscious effort is necessary which will enable the two octaves to continue their development. The nature of this effort demands special study. From the point of view of the general work of the machine it can be said in general that this effort is connected with the emotional life, that it is a special kind of influence over one's emotions. But what this kind of influence really is, and how it has to be produced, can be explained only in connection with a general description of the work of the human factory or the human machine…
>
> "… The nature of this second 'shock' cannot be so easily described as the nature of the first volitional 'shock' at do 48. In order to understand the nature of this 'shock' it is necessary to understand the meaning of si 12 and mi 12.
>
> "The effort which creates this 'shock' must consist in work on the emotions, in the transformation and transmutation of the emotions. This transmutation of the emotions will then help the transmutation of si 12 in the human organism. No serious growth, that is no growth of higher bodies within the organism, is possible without this transmutation. The idea of this transmutation was known to many ancient teachings as well as to some comparatively recent ones, such as the alchemy of the Middle Ages … .

---

60 Gurdjieff, *Beelzebub's Tales*, pp 753-54.

"... Right development on the fourth way must begin with the first volitional 'shock' and then pass on to the second 'shock' at mi 12 [the mi 12–fa 6 interval].

"The third stage in the work of the human organism begins when man creates in himself a conscious second volitional 'shock' at the point mi12, when the transformation or transmutation of these 'hydrogens' into higher 'hydrogens' begins in him. The second stage and the beginning of the third stage refer to the life and functions of man number four. A fairly considerable period of transmutation and crystallization is needed for the transition of man number four to the level of man number five."[61]

Illustration 12 combines, in symbolic terms, a number of the points that are emphasized in the previous quotations.

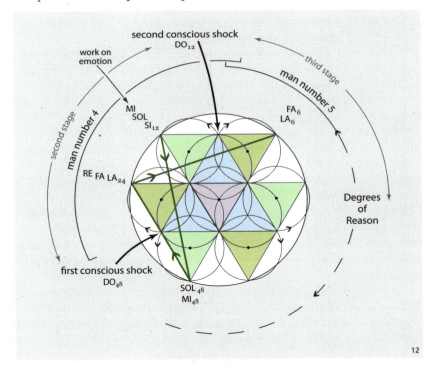

12

The understanding of the meaning of SI_{12}, SOL_{12} and MI_{12} is, as Ouspensky noted, the key to understanding the nature of the second *conscious* shock. In the chapter "Gurdjieff's 'hydrogens'" in *Perspectives*,[62] we posited that the category of material/vibrations called 'hydrogen' 12 was composed of light

---

[61] Ouspensky, *In Search*, pp 191-93.
[62] Buzzell, *Perspectives on Beelzebub's Tales*, chapter 9, "Gurdjieff's 'hydrogens'," and *Explorations*, chapter 11, "Gurdjieff's Creation Myth," pp 115-16.

waves or photons.[63] Photons, as the 'carriers' of the electromagnetic force, while being without charge themselves, simultaneously mediate positive and negative charge. This triadic nature, possessing positive (active), negative (passive) and neutral (reconciling) attributes, is resonant with the powers we have attributed to *attention*, namely — "to focus" (*making 1s*) — "to divide" or differentiate (*making 2s*) — and "to order" (*making 3s*).[64]

ATTENTION AND CONSCIOUSNESS

From this perspective, attention and 'waking' consciousness (Gurdjieff's second state of consciousness) are expressions of quite different material/vibrations. Waking (or ordinary) consciousness is a basal state of awareness, which is present in all sentient beings. It is like a screen upon which the images deriving from the sensory input to the three brains are projected.

While the SI_{12} of physical food produced is automatic attention, the MI_{12} and the SOL_{12} is never automatic but involves the use or the application of the Will (the directed attention).

Attention is a power (with three aspects), quite different in its nature from the basal state of consciousness. It is like a beam of light which can be directed upon portions of the screen. In the initial stages of its action, it is the power "to focus" (*to make 1s*). If the attention is held on one region of the 'screen' of waking consciousness, a differentiation (*to make 2s*) begins to take place; differences are noticed. These may be differences (or nuances) in feeling, in sensation or in words/ideas, depending on which brains' images (or combinations of them) have been focused upon. All share the essential characteristic of being taken apart (divided) from the state of the initial 'one' that was focused upon.

If the attention continues to be held on this now differentiated or divided region of waking consciousness, one begins to 'see' relationships (*to make 3s*) between or among the separated parts. These three powers will unfold, rapidly and quite naturally, if the attention is consistently applied to the impression.

This unfolding of the triadic powers of attention occurs even in the second state of consciousness, but is not consistently applied because it lacks the directive aspect present in the state of self-remembering. Many nuances and further points of differentiation are made in the third state of consciousness and the arenas of potential relationships are greatly expanded.

---

63 The wavelength of photons (which reflects their frequency in vibrations/sec) varies over an incredibly large range. At the low energy end of the spectrum, wavelengths can be greater than (10^8 meters (1,000,000,000 meters or 621,000 miles), whereas at the high end wavelengths can be shorter than 10^{-24} meters (0.000000000000000000000001 meters). The frequency ranges produced by human brain activity are in the range of 0.5–100 vibrations/sec (extremely low frequency or ELF waves). At these frequencies, photons have almost no energy but are traveling at 186,000 miles/sec.

64 Buzzell, *Explorations*, chapter 11, "Gurdjieff's Creation Myth," pp 93-95.

Attention drives the brain's inherent neural processes which search for meaning and significance.[65] "Meaning," in this context, is the product of the third power of attention (*creating 3s* or a pattern/order). When attention is brought to bear on any of the three brain's images (or portions of them), the associative cortex of that brain (whether thinking, feeling or sensory-motion) is stimulated to undertake a search (or 'hunt') for the meaning of that image. As noted, the first brain will immediately undertake an evaluation as to whether the image is a resonant representation of a mate, a possible source of food, a possible adversary or simply a part of the landscape, (e.g., a tree branch or a rock). If no meaning (in a survival context) is found, the second brain will, slightly later (in neural time), undertake an exploration of the image with *relationship* as its underpinning principle. Depending on whether the image is of a relative, acquaintance, associate or stranger, the searched for meaning will focus on the present moment status of the relationship, (e.g., in need of nurture, an expression of irritability, giving direction, companionability, etc.). Slightly later (in the neurological time of micro-seconds), the thinking brain will undertake its search, naming the images and their parts, abstracting ideas, analyzing possibilities, justifying the feeling state in its characteristic 'waking-consciousness state' and 'indulging in perpetual chatter'.

In each of the three brains, all of this associative activity takes place automatically, activated by an attention that in turn is initiated by instinctive and social survival mechanisms that have appeared within each brain.

In sharp contrast, directing the attention (with an inner separation established) is a *conscious* effort, intimately related to the third state of consciousness. It is free of the automaticities that derive from instinctive center function and the Itoklanoz-conditioned personality. Because it is held separate from the images of the three brains, it can direct a far more impartial 'hunt' for meanings. To varying degrees (increasing with repeated efforts), the triadic nature of the images is seen into; their origins and dependencies on the past being clarified, with new and deeper meanings appearing. With increasing clarity, the mechanicalness of one's 'life of personality' is laid bare. Simultaneously, (empowered by group work and the sharing of impressions), one comes to see and accept that other people are equally mechanical.[66] Slowly, the personality processes leading to justification, lying, hiding and other egoistic expressions are more and more exposed and, in consequence, progressively devalued. The 'hot scald' of the remorse of conscience slowly lays bare the self-created 'constructions' which are the crystallized consequences of the properties of the organ Kundabuffer. Other efforts of Work (including following the breath, sensing, tasks and exercises, Movements and music study) blend with these efforts to see more deeply into oneself and offer, at this critical juncture of $MI_{12}-SOL_{12}-SI_{12}$, assistance in the effort TO BE and the effort to create new ways of feeling, thinking and manifesting.

---

[65] Refer to chapter 2, where a brain as a 'hunter' is discussed PP 48-59 in this volume and *Explorations*, chapter 6, "Image as Man's Three-brained Reality."

[66] See the story of Belcultasssi in *The Tales*, P 296.

This is a highly experimental stage, demanding of creativity, spontaneity and risk-taking, because one is not yet totally free of the past and all of its encumbrances and still not able to stand fully in one's *being*.

The MI_{12} level of material vibrations refers to the directed attention enabling the intellect to explore and come to deeper meanings regarding cosmic law (Heptaparaparshinokh, Triamazikamno, second-degree and other laws), while, simultaneously, at SOL_{12}, the feeling world of right relationships and values toward and for all others (the manifestations of real conscience) is seen and striven toward. The "special study" regarding the emotional life which Gurdjieff refers to in the opening quotation of this segment is intimately related to this action at SOL_{12}.

We understand that aspects of SI_{12} (physical-generative material vibrations)[67] are involved in work on the Movements and Sacred Dances. These material vibrations can evoke and support the creative expression of laws that are symbolized or abstracted in bodily form. As such, they are very high 'hydrogens' (food) for all three brains as well as powerful enabling influences in work on *being*.

To speak of MI_{12}, SOL_{12}, SI_{12} as separate aspects of Fourth Way work is not really correct. The work of man number four is the work of man number one, two or three, making the efforts to become a *balanced* man. As such, any aspect of work influences, enables and/or creates tensions in other aspects of work. A higher 'hydrogen' entering from outside or from an inner work effort, may dramatically influence a number of related lower 'hydrogen' states. In all of this, however, directed attention (H_{12}–H_6) is the singular reconciling influence that enables the emergence of true balance.

THE SECOND *CONSCIOUS* SHOCK

In the opening quotation of the previous segment, Gurdjieff said, referring to the second *conscious* shock, "the nature of this effort demands special study." We are not competent or sufficiently experienced to consider what this "special study" would encompass, but would underscore, again, the importance of the simultaneity and relationship of the three octaves and their changed intervals — the mechano-coinciding-Mdnel-In, the Harnel-Aoot and the intentionally-actualized-Mdnel-In. The passage through each interval contributes uniquely to the circumstance into which the second *conscious* shock enters.

In *In Search*, Gurdjieff is quoted as saying, "I will say that, if you like, *this is esoteric Christianity*. We will talk in due course about the meaning of these words."[68] The literature on esoteric Christianity has expanded considerably since the discovery of many ancient texts, most notably the Dead Sea scrolls and the Nag Hammadi library. Among the studies and commentaries

---

67 In half-awake man, the procreative SI_{12} category of material vibrations is utilized only for sexual reproduction.
68 Ouspensky, *In Search*, P 102.

that have been published recently, there is one, *Inner Christianity* by Richard Smoley, that contains a reference to what we understand as one core aspect of the second *conscious* shock. We will end our exploration of the initial stages of self-transformation with that reference.

> "Up to now this book has spoken of the "I" in referring to the spirit of consciousness that is the true Self. And this is correct: this principle is that in each of us which says "I" at the deepest level possible, beyond all thought and desire and even beyond ordinary waking consciousness. But if one stops at this point, a cosmic egotism springs up, a spiritual pride that is the deadliest of the Seven Deadly Sins. Legend even says that Lucifer fell because he dared to say "I" in the presence of the Holy One.
>
> Following the way of inner Christianity to its full conclusion means stepping past the constraints of the "I," which in its turn must take its rightful place in the cosmic order. And this requires an awareness of the central mystery of Christianity, which could rightly be said to enable one to "enter into the Kingdom of God."
>
> It is simply this: *The "I" is ultimately the same in all of us.* We are collectively one great being, the Son of God which is known in its fallen state as Adam and its unified state as Christ."[69]

A QUALIFICATION

Our aim in this book has been to blend a scientific perspective on the physical Universe and on human biology with a perspective on the possibility of self-transformation as taught by G. I. Gurdjieff. Because it is verbal in form, it can do little more than hint, or metaphorically point toward, the broad spectrum of human experiences that must be personally *lived* in order to have its full meaning. Chapter 4 is an intellectual 'scratch' on the surface of the body of real Work, hopefully inviting the reader to probe deeper and to explore possible connections to groups that are actively engaged in the practice of the Gurdjieff teaching. Because we are all together in this adventure of life on earth, we need to share, to commune with, to support and to come into abiding relationship with each other.

---

69 Richard Smoley, *Inner Christianity: A Guide to the Esoteric Tradition* (Boston: Shambhala Publications, 2002), P 96.

CHAPTER 4 PAGES 88 AND 90 ENDNOTES
 I Gurdjieff, *Beelzebub's Tales*, P 769.
 II Ibid., P 1172.
 III Harrington, *The Dalai Lama at MIT*, P 100, comment by Alan Wallace.
 IV Goddard, *A Buddhist Bible*, P 308, quoting Buddha.
 V Ibid.
 VI Ouspensky, *In Search*, P 117.

"We must be clear that, when it comes to atoms, language can be used only as in poetry."[1]

"A human being ... experiences himself, his thoughts and feelings as something separated from the rest — a kind of optical illusion of his consciousness. This delusion is a kind of prison for us, restricting us to our personal desires and to affection for a few persons nearest to us. Our task must be to free ourselves from this prison by widening our circle of understanding and compassion to embrace all living creatures and the whole of nature in its beauty."[2]

---

[1] Niels Bohr, *The Philosophical Writings of Niels Bohr*, Volume 1 (Woodbridge: Ox Bow Press, 1987), P 54.
[2] Alice Calaprice, ed., *The Expandable Quotable Einstein* (Princeton: Princeton University Press, 2000) quoting Albert Einstein.

Glossary

ALEPH 0, 1, 2 ~ three distinct infinities discovered by George Cantor

AFFERENT/EFFERENT ~ input/output for the nervous system

ANGSTRÖM ~ a unit of length equal to 10^{-8} cm

ANTHROPOCENTRIC ~ man as the central aspect of the universe

ARCHAEBACTERIA ~ primitive micro-organisms including methane-producing forms, some red halophilic forms and others of harsh hot acidic environments

ATP ~ (called also adenosine triphosphate) the most efficient form of storage of high energy phosphate bonds in the biological cell

BEING-OBLIGOLNIAN-STRIVINGS ~ [*Beelzebub's Tales*, P 386]

> "The first striving: to have in their ordinary being-existence everything satisfying and really necessary for their planetary body.
>
> "The second striving: to have a constant and unflagging instinctive need for self-perfection in the sense of being.
>
> "The third: the conscious striving to know ever more and more concerning the laws of World-creation and World-maintenance.
>
> "The fourth: the striving from the beginning of their existence to pay for their arising and their individuality as quickly as possible, in order afterwards to be free to lighten as much as possible the Sorrow of our COMMON FATHER.
>
> "And the fifth: the striving always to assist the most rapid perfecting of other beings, both those similar to oneself and those of other forms, up to the degree of the sacred 'Martfotai' that is up to the degree of self-individuality."

BOSON CARRIERS ~ a particle that carries one of the fundamental forces between other interacting particles.

CATIONS AND ANIONS ~ ions with a positive (cat) or negative (an) charge.

EXTEROCEPTIVE ~ a sense organ of the skin which is activated by stimuli received from outside

FAMILY TRIAD ~ an expression coined by Dr. Paul MacLean referring to the appearance of nurture, audio-vocal communication and play behaviors as the core aspect of mammalian life

GANGLIONIC ~ a general term designating a group of nerve cell bodies located outside of the central nervous system

GENOME ~ the complete set of hereditary factors, as contained in the haploid assortment of chromosomes

HARNEL-AOOT ~ the changed fifth deflection of the sacred Heptaparaparshinokh (Law of Seven) [*Beelzebub's Tales*, P 758]

HARNEL-MIA[T]ZNEL ~ [*Beelzebub's Tales*, P 751]

> "… the process of which is actualized thus: the higher blends with the lower in order to actualize the middle and thus becomes either higher for the preceding lower, or lower for the succeeding higher …"

HIPPOCAMPUS, AMYGDALA, HYPOTHALAMUS AND CINGULATE GYRUS ~ cerebral centers that are primary aspects of the second brain.

INTERNUNCIAL ~ serving as a medium of communication between nerve neurons or centers

INTEROCEPTIVE ~ a specialized cell or end organ that responds to and transmits stimuli from the internal organs, muscles, blood vessels and the ear organs

MASTER ROUTINES AND SUBROUTINES ~ biologically driven absolutely primary behaviors in one-brained creatures, e.g., display, feeding, mating, defensive postures ~ subroutine: less important; variable

MECHANO-COINCIDING-MDNEL-IN ~ the lengthened Stopinder between the third and fourth deflections of the sacred Heptaparaparshinokh [*Beelzebub's Tales*, pp 753-54]

MECHANORECEPTORS ~ specialized nerve receptors that are sensitive to mechanical pressure

MENSURATION ~ measurement

MOTOR EFFERENT ~ axon (nerve fiber) leading from a nerve cell to muscular tissue

MUSCLE SPINDLE (GAMMA SYSTEM) ~ secondary muscular innervation controlling small groups of muscle fibers with respect to tone

NEURAL NET ~ dense network of nerve cells

NEURAL ASSEMBLY ~ an organized group of nerve cells serving a specific function

NUCLEOSYNTHESIS ~ the production of a chemical element from simpler nuclei (as of hydrogen) especially in a star

PERISTALSIS ~ consists of a wave of contraction passing along the intestinal tube

PIEZOELECTRIC PRINCIPLE ~ property of some crystals (e.g., quartz) of acquiring opposite electrical charges on opposing surfaces when subjected to pressure

PROPRIOCEPTORS ~ a sensory receptor (as a muscle spindle) excited by proprioceptive stimuli (as changes in limb position)

PROTOMENTATION ~ mentation of the physical body

RESONANT REPRESENTATION ~ an image

R-COMPLEX ~ highest part of the first brain.

STEREOTACTIC ~ three-dimensional location of a point

VILLI ~ minute processes that project outward from the lining of the small intestine

VISCERA ~ internal organs of the body

Recommended Reading — References

Ackerman, Diane. *A Natural History of the Senses*.
   New York: Random House, 1990.
Barrow, John. *Theories of Everything*.
   New York: Oxford University Press, 2007.
Bronowski, Jacob. *The Ascent of Man*. Toronto: Little, Brown and Co., 1974.
Bohm, David. *The Ending of Time*. New York: Harper & Row, 1980.
   Wholeness and the Implicate Order. London: Routledge & Kegan Paul, 1980.
Bohr, Niels. *The Philosophical Writings of Niels Bohr*, Volume 2.
   Woodbridge: Ox Bow Press, 1987.
Buzzell, Keith A. *The Children of Cyclops: The Influence of Television Viewing on the Developing Brain*. Fair Oaks: AWSNA Publications, 1998.
   Perspectives on Beelzebub's Tales. Salt Lake City: Fifth Press, 2005.
   Explorations in Active Mentation. Salt Lake City: Fifth Press, 2006.
Calaprice, Alice, editor. *The Expandable Quotable Einstein*.
   Princeton: Princeton University Press, 2000.
Cantor, George. *Contributions to the Founding of the Theory of Transfinite Numbers*. Philip Jourdain, ed. and trans. Dover, 1955. Cantor published many complex mathematical papers in the early decades of the 20th century.
Changeux, Jean-Pierre. "Chemical Signaling in the Brain." *Scientific American* (November 1993), 58-62.
Cooper, Jack, R., Floyd E. Bloom, Robert H. Roth. *The Biochemical Basis of Neuropharmacology*. New York: Oxford University Press, 1991.
Coppens, Yves. "East Side Story: The Origin of Humankind." *Scientific American* (May 1994), 88-95.
Dalai Lama, H.H. *The Universe in a Single Atom: The Convergence of Science and Spirituality*. New York: Morgan Road Books, 2005.
DeArmond, Stephen T., Madeline M. Fusco and Maynard M. Dewey. *Structure of the Human Brain*. New York: Oxford University Press, 1989.
DeDuve, Christian. *Vital Dust, Life as a Cosmic Imperative*.
   New York: Basic Books, 1995.
Eddington, Sir Arthur. *The Nature of the Physical World*. New York: MacMillan Co., 1928.
Einstein, Albert. *Out of My Later Years*. New York: Philosophical Library, 1950.
Goddard, Dwight, editor. *A Buddhist Bible*. Boston: Beacon Press, 1932.
Guide and Index to G.I. Gurdjieff's Beelzebub's Tales to His Grandson.
   Louise M. Welch, editor. Toronto: Traditional Studies Press, 2003.
Gurdjieff, George Ivanovitch.
   All and Everything/First Series. "An Objectively Impartial Criticism of the Life of Man" or *Beelzebub's Tales to His Grandson*.
      Facsimile republication. Aurora: Two Rivers Press, 1993;
      and New York: Penguin Arkana, 1999.

  Meetings with Remarkable Men, All and Everything/Second Series.
   New York: Penguin Books, 1991.
  Life is real only then, when "I am," All and Everything/Third Series.
   New York: Penguin Books, 1999.
  Views from the Real World: Early Talks of Gurdjieff.
   New York: Penguin Books, 1991.
  Herald of Coming Good. New York: Samuel Weiser, 1973.
Harrington, Anne, editor.
  The Dalai Lama at MIT. Cambridge: Harvard University Press, 2006.
Heap, Jane. *The Notes of Jane Heap.* Aurora: Two Rivers Press, 1994.
  Jane Heap/Notes. Aurora: Two Rivers Press, 1983.
Hooper, Judith and Dick Teresi. *The 3-Pound Universe.*
  New York: MacMillan Co., 1986.
Kalin, Ned H."The Neurobiology of Fear." *Scientific American*
  (May 1993), 94-101.
Kimhi, Joseph. *Shekel Hakodesh, The Holy Shekel.*
  Whitefish: Kessinger Publishing, 2007.
MacFadden, Johnjoe. *Quantum Evolution.* New York: W.W. Norton, 2000.
MacLean, Paul D. *The Triune Brain in Evolution: Role in Paleocerebral*
  Functions. New York: Plenum Press, 1990.
Moyzis, Robert K. "The Human Telomere." *Scientific American*
  (August 1991), 48-55.
Murchie, Guy. *The Seven Mysteries of Life.*
  Boston: Houghton Mifflin Co., 1978.
Nicoll, Maurice. *Psychological Commentaries on the Teaching of G.I.*
  Gurdjieff and P.D. Ouspensky. York Beach: Weiser, 1996.
Orage, A.R. *A.R. Orage's Commentaries on G.I. Gurdjieff's All and*
  Everything: Beelzebub's Tales to His Grandson. C.S. Nott, editor. Aurora:
  Two Rivers Press, 1985.
  Psychological Exercises and Essays. New York: Samuel Weiser, 1974.
Ouspensky, P.D. *In Search of the Miraculous.* San Diego: Harvest/HBJ
  Book, 2001.
  The Psychology of Man's Possible Evolution. New York: Vintage Books, 1974.
Pearce, Joseph Chilton. *Evolution's End: Changing the Potential of Our*
  Intelligence. San Francisco: Harper, 1992.
Penfield, Wilder. *The Mystery of the Mind.* Princeton: Princeton University
  Press, 1975.
Pert, Candace. "Opiate Receptor: Demonstration in Nervous Tissue."
  Science Magazine (179, 1973), 1011-1014.
Popoff, Irmis B. *Gurdjieff Group Work with Wilhem Nyland.*
  York Beach: Weiser, 1983.
  Gurdjieff: His Work on Myself, With Others, For the Work.
  New York: Vantage Press, 1969.

Pribram, Karl H. *Languages of the Brain: Experimental Paradoxes and Principles in Neuropsychology.* Englewood Cliffs: Prentice-Hall, 1971.

Schumacher, E. F. *Small is Beautiful.* Point Roberts: Hartley & Marks, 1999.

Shepherd, Gordon. *Neurobiology.* Oxford: Oxford University Press, 1983.

Smoley, Richard. *Inner Christianity: A Guide to the Esoteric Tradition.* Boston: Shambhala Publications, 2002.

Staveley, A. L. *Themes I.* Aurora: Two Rivers Press, 1981.

Taylor, Paul Beekman. *Gurdjieff's America: Mediating the Miraculous.* London: Lighthouse Editions, 2004.

Tracol, Henri. *George Ivanovich Gurdjieff: Man's Awakening and the Practice of Remembering Oneself.* London: Pembridge Design Studio Press, 1987.

Waldrop, M. Mitchell. *Complexity: The Emerging Science at the Edge of Order and Chaos.* New York: Simon & Schuster, 1992.

Weber, Renee. *Dialogues with Scientists and Sages: The Search for Unity.* London: Routledge & Kegan Paul, 1986.

Wilber, Ken, editor. *The Holographic Paradigm and Other Paradoxes.* Boston: Shambhala Publications, 1982.

Wilson, Allan C. and Rebecca L. Cann. "The Recent African Genesis of Humans." *Scientific American* (April 1992), 68-73.

Young, Arthur. *The Geometry of Meaning.*
    Mill Valley: Robert Briggs, Associates, 1976.
The Reflexive Universe. Mill Valley: Robert Briggs, Associates, 1976.

KEITH A. BUZZELL, A.B., D.O.

Dr. Buzzell was born in 1932 in Boston, Massachusetts. He studied music at Bowdoin College and Boston University and received his medical doctorate in 1960 at the Philadelphia College of Osteopathic Medicine. Dr. Buzzell served as a hospital medical director, a professor of osteopathic medicine and was the founder of the Western Maine hospice program. He has lectured widely on the neuro-physiological influences of television on the developing human brain and on the evolution of man's triune brain. For the past thirty eight years, he has been a rural family physician in Fryeburg, Maine, a staff member of Bridgton Hospital and currently holds the position of medical director at the Fryeburg Health Care Center.

In 1971, Keith and his wife, Marlena, became students of Irmis Popoff, who herself was a student of Gurdjieff and Ouspensky and founder of the Pinnacle Group in Sea Cliff, Long Island, New York. From then until the mid-1980s, they formed Work groups under her supervision. In 1988, they met Annie Lou Staveley, founder of Two Rivers Farm in Oregon, and maintained a Work relationship with her up to her death.

Keith has given presentations at the All and Everything International Humanities Conferences 1995-2007, which are published in the annual Conference Proceedings (www.aandeconference.org). Keith and Marlena live and continue group Work in Bridgton, Maine.

Acknowledgements
Carol Sogard – book design
Pam Woodmansee – book production
Ed Bateman – graphic illustration
E. Louise Merrill – manuscript preparation
Steve Bruun – Artistic Printing
Tay Haines – administrative assistant
Stephen Seko – administrative assistant

With Gratitude
Keith Badger
Pat and Harry Bennett
Ocke de Boer
Elizabeth and James Evans
Larry Forbes
Colin R. Hebb
Bruce Kennett
George Pfender
Paul Taylor
The Staff at Phillips Gallery

Artwork
Drawing of Dr. Keith A. Buzzell by Julian Maack
Frontispiece, dedication and page 9 by Bonnie Phillips

Colophon
This book was set in New Caledonia designed by William A. Dwiggins, issued in digital form by Linotype, Bad Homburg, Germany in 1982. Text for illustrations is set in Frutiger and New Caledonia. Frutiger was designed by Adrian Frutiger, issued by D. Stempel A.G. in conjunction with Linotype Library in 1976. The paper is Mohawk VIA White Smooth, seventy pound, one hundred percent post-consumer waste.

Back Cover Quote
Gurdjieff, *Beelzebub's Tales*, p 769.